3

AMERICAN GRAPHIC DESIGN AWARDS
No. 4

Copyright © 2004 by Kaye Publishing Corp.

Visual Reference Publications, Inc.
302 Fifth Avenue
New York, Y 10001

Distributors to the trade in the United States and Canada:
Watson-Guptill
770 Broadway
New York, NY 10003

Distributors outside of the United States and Canada:
HarperCollins International
10 East 53rd Street
New York, NY 10022

Library of Congress Cataloging in Publication Data:
American Graphic Design Awards No. 4
Printed in China
ISBN 1-58471-076-4

CONTENTS

We conclude our 40th anniversary of publishing Graphic Design usa on a high note, by inviting you to view our Annual. This edition showcases a select handful of the more than 10,000 entries in this year's competition.

Recently, we commissioned independent readership studies to make sure Graphic Design usa is on track. The results on traditional measures of readership have been very gratifying. Even more pleasing to me are the responses to more emotional, less traditional questions. Graphic design professionals rank us first in well-rounded coverage of all types of creative firms and projects, rather than just the rich and famous; for serving to connect the community and fostering a shared identity; and for being just plain friendly and accessible.

The key to the explosive growth of our awards program lies in those findings.

The winners represent many of the great creative minds and organizations of our time, as well as many striving to excel and gain recognition. Projects run the gamut from traditional collateral to sexy new media, from dream assignments to bread-and-butter endeavors, from Fortune 500 annual reports to nonprofit public service postcards, from hardworking packaging to glossy fashion magazines. Entrants come from the largest of cities, the smallest of towns, the most suburban of ... well, suburbs.

The point is that the competition, like the magazine which sponsors it, is a metaphorical "big tent" — open, accessible and ever more representative of the many and diverse ways in which graphic design shapes and interprets commerce and culture.

I have a good feeling that 2004 will see a resurgence of energy, focus and prosperity in the creative community. After you review this Annual, you will feel that way too.

Gordon Kaye, Editor and Publisher

On Behalf of
Laura Roth, Awards Director
Milton Kaye, Associate Awards Director
Ilana Greenberg, Art Director
Rachel Goldberg, Production Manager
Bradley H. Kerr, Associate Editor

...

JUDGES

A special thanks to our extraordinary panel of talented creative professionals from all over the country who served a judges for the 2003 American Graphic Design Awards.

LYNDA DECKER

Lynda Decker is the visionary engine that directs the work created at Decker Design. For 20 years, she has been involved in advertising, direct marketing, publication design, corporate identity, collateral, corporate publication systems and electronic media. Decker began her career under the legendary tutelage of Herb Lubalin, Seymour Chwast and Alan Peckolick at Pushpin Lubalin Peckolick. She then did award-winning work at McCaffrey and McCall Direct on assignments for Mercedes Benz, T. Rowe Price and Falcon Jet. From there she went to Backer Spielvogel Bates, to design collateral for CBS. Next, joining Wells Rich Greene BDDP as senior design director, Decker designed IBM's domestic corporate collateral. She then worked as creative director at Downey Weeks & Toomey, until deciding to throw caution to the wind and open her own shop in New York City. An active member of AIGA/NY, Decker recently completed a two year tenure as vice president and board member.

RICHARD HOLLANT

For over 15 years, Richard Hollant has launched products and services "around the world, using every communications medium at his disposal." The founder and director of co:lab, based in Hartford CT, his work for clients including Travelers/Citicorp, ConAgra Foods, Motorola, Harley Davidson, Mohawk Papers and Zygmo Records has garnered awards and yielded results. Hollant lectures on the Zen of Design, and is at work on a book about design as an empirical process. He started a mentoring program for design students, and is forming a collection of photo-based iconographs. In his spare time, Hollant is a singer/songwriter/guitarist for a groove-based folk rock band.

RANI LEVY

Creative director Rani Levy oversees the design, layout and photography of Graphic Arts Monthly, the trade magazine for commercial printers published by Reed Business Information. Responsible for the magazine's visual appeal, her goal is to make artwork an integral part of its editorial presentation. Levy launched and managed the art direction of Digital Design & Production and Quick Print Products. Before that, she worked at Windows, Brides Magazine and Omni, where her publication design efforts garnered several awards.

BILL PAETZOLD

Bill Paetzold founded Paetzold Associates, a multidisciplinary visual communications firm specializing in consumer packaging, corporate branding, identity systems, collateral, web animation and cutting-edge interactive media. Under Paetzold's creative direction, the the firm's blend of compelling design and effective marketing has attracted major retailers, service providers, financial institutions, publishers, sporting goods manufacturers, music producers and not-for profit organizations, including the likes of Sears, Suncast, Aramark and The Special Olympics. Prior to its founding, Paetzold held several high-level design and management positions, including creative director for a major publisher. He has also graced the January 2002 cover of Graphic Design usa. Paetzold Associates is based in St. Charles IL.

STEVE PERRY

Steve Perry is a group design director at The Bailey Group where is responsible for the art direction and management of the studio's creative team. A graduate of Penn State, with over a dozen years of experience in brand development, identity and package design, he has he worked on strategic branding programs for Maxell, Welch's, Marriot and Johnson & Johnson, among others. Perry's work has been featured in Communication Arts, Graphic Design usa, How, Print and Step-By-Step. Plymouth Meeting PA is the home of The Bailey Group.

ROCCO PISCATELLO

Rocco Piscatello founded the New York City-based Piscatello Design Centre, a multidisciplinary firm that creates identities, environmental graphics and interactive design systems for a broad range of cultural and corporate clients. Piscatello recently lead the team that designed the identity and environmental graphics for the Irish Hunger Memorial in New York's Battery Park City. He was also involved in developing an innovative design proposal with architect Richard Meier for the future World Trade Center site, and completed an interactive web site for the 150 year old furniture company Bernhardt Design. Prior to forming his own firm, Piscatello worked for Vignelli Associates. He also teaches design an advanced typography at the Fashion Institute of Technology.

ELAINE TAJIMA

Elaine Tajima is the founder/president/ceo of Tajima Creative, a visual communications and marketing services company serving a diverse range of clients including Washington Mutual, Warner Brothers and AirWave from her office in Menlo Park CA. She studied goldsmithing at Cal State-Long Beach. After college she worked as a Pasadena Rose Parade Float Builder, which gave birth to a lifelong passion for design. She became a freelance fashion stylist for May Dept. Stores, and rose to serve as creative director for visual merchandising. Liz Claiborne's First Issue brought her to New York in the 80s and Dayton Hudson lured her to direct Mervyn's instore marketing. She founded her own award-winning firm in 1996. Tajima has curated traveling art exhibitionsand serves on the board of the Palo Alto Art Center Foundation. She lives in Palo Alto and has a daughter.

GREGORY THOMAS

Gregory Thomas is the owner/founding principal of Gregory Thomas Associates (GTA), a studio specializing in corporate communications literature and direct response materials. Clients include CBS, IBM, Federal Reserve Bank of San Francisco, Seagram's and the nations of Australia, New Zealand and Austria. The firm is in the process of branding the City of Alhambra CA and developing a signage program for USC. The more than 25 year old firm has won national and international awards, and has been featured or quoted in a variety of publications. Thomas is also an adjunct professor at the School of Fine Arts and the Annenberg School For Communication at USC. He is a prolific author, and is on the advisory board of Designer, the publication of the University and College Designer Assoc. Prior to his work for Charles & Ray Eames and Saul Bass, Thomas studied at Kansas City Art Institute (BFA), Cal. Institute of Arts (MFA) and Yale (MFA).

DAVE ZAMBOTTI

Dave Zambotti is co-founder of Zamboo, a full-service creative agency providing results-driven graphic design, technology and marketing solutions. His designs for Apple Computer, Toyota, Dogloo and the Blue Cross of California, among others, have garnered numerous national awards. "Awards are great," he opines, "but I'm more interested in design the gets results."

ANNUAL REPORTS

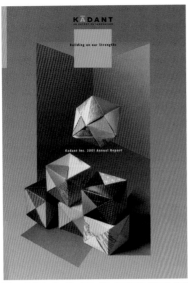

Design Firm: 2 Hats Design Ltd., Wayland MA **Client:** Kadant Inc.
Title: Annual Report **Art Directors:** Anne Scheer, Dotti Cullinan **Designers:** Anne Scheer, Dotti Cullinan **Photographer:** John Earle

Design Firm: ACME Design Group, Newton PA **Client:** Young Audiences
Title: Annual Report **Art Director:** John Mulvaney **Designers:** John Mulvaney, Justin Moll **Illustrator:** Sarah Wilkens **Photographer:** Peter Olson

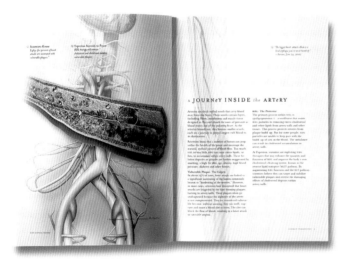

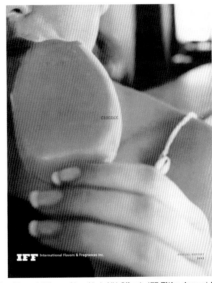

Design Firm: ACME Design Group, Newton PA **Client:** Esperion
Title: Annual Report **Art Director:** Justin Moll **Designer:** Justin Moll
Illustrator: Keith Kasnot **Photographer:** Ron Brello Jr.

Design Firm: Addison, New York NY **Client:** IFF **Title:** Annual Report
Art Directors: Chris Korbey, Richard Colbourne **Photographers:** Various

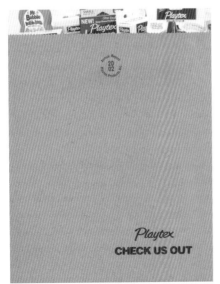

Design Firm: Addison, New York NY **Client:** Playtex Products
Title: Annual Report **Creative Director:** David Kohler **Designer:** Michelle Aptman **Photographer:** Dan Bigelow Photography

Design Firm: Addison, New York NY **Client:** iStar Financial **Title:** Annual Report
Art Directors: Christina Antonopoulus, Richard Colbourne

Design Firm: Addison, New York NY Client: Wilmington Trust Corporation
Title: Annual Report Creative Director: David Kohler Designer: John Moon
Photographers: Scott Hewitt and various

Design Firm: Addison, New York NY Client: Intelsat
Title: Annual Report Art Director: David Kohler Designer: Rick Slusher
Photographer: Dan Bigelow Photography

Design Firm: Addison, New York NY Client: CP Ships Title: Annual Report
Art Director: Christina Antonopoulus Designer: Christina Antonopoulus
Illustrator: Kai Wiechmann Photographer: Kai Wiechmann

Design Firm: ART 270, Jenkintown PA Client: AmerisourceBergen
Corporation Title: Annual Report Art Director: Carl Mill Designers: Sue Strohm,
John Opet Photographer: Jerome Lukowicz

Design Firm: ART 270, Jenkintown PA Client: Sanchez Computer
Associates Title: Annual Report Art Director: Carl Mill Designer: John Opet
Photographer: Jerome Lukowicz

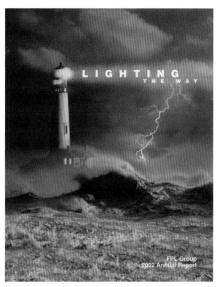

Design Firm: ART 270, Jenkintown PA Client: FPL Group
Title: Annual Report Art Director: Carl Mill Designers: Nicole
Ganz, John Opet Photographer: Craig Bromley

Design Firm: ART 270, Jenkintown PA **Client:** Natural Lands Trust
Title: Progress Report **Art Director:** Carl Mill **Designer:** Nicole Ganz

Design Firm: Baltimore Area Convention and Visitors Association (BACVA),
Baltimore MD **Title:** BACVA Annual Report **Designer:** Georganne Cammarata

Design Firm: Blue Shield of California, San Francisco CA **Title:** Report to
Californians **Art Director:** Stephanie Donahue **Designer:** Stephanie Donahue
Photographer: Sybilla Herbich

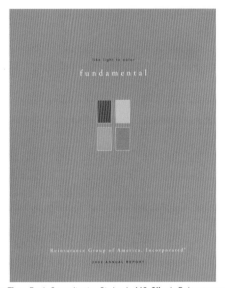

Design Firm: Buck Consultants, St. Louis MO **Client:** Reinsurance Group
of America **Title:** Annual Report **Art Director:** Stan Sams **Designer:** Jennifer
Sagaser **Photographers:** Anthony Arciero, Greg Rannells

Design Firm: Cahan and Associates, San Francisco CA **Client:** Yellow
Title: Annual Report **Art Director:** Bill Cahan **Designer:** Sharrie Brooks
Photographers: Todd Hido, Ron Coppock-King

Design Firm: Cahan and Associates, San Francisco CA **Client:** Charles
Schwab **Title:** Annual Report **Art Directors:** Bill Cahan, Sharrie Brooks
Designer: Sharrie Brooks **Photographer:** Fergus Greer

Design Firm: Cahan and Associates, San Francisco CA
Client: BRE Properties **Title:** 2002 Annual Report **Art Directors:** Bill Cahan, Bob Dinetz **Designer:** Bob Dinetz **Photographer:** Todd Hido

Design Firm: Cahan and Associates, San Francisco CA
Client: Levi Strauss **Title:** Annual Report **Art Director:** Bill Cahan
Designer: Gary Williams **Photographer:** Todd Hido

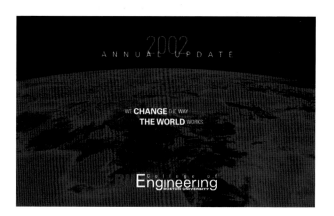

Design Firm: Christina Balas, Long Branch NJ **Client:** Georgian Court College
Title: Annual Report **Designer:** Christina Balas

Design Firm: Cisneros Design, Santa Fe NM **Client:** Santa Fe Children's Museum **Title:** Annual Report **Art Director:** Brian Hurshman
Designer: Yvette Jones **Photographer:** Scott Plunket

Design Firm: Crocker & Company, Hamilton MA **Client:** Boston University Division of Extended Education **Title:** Annual Report **Designer:** Peter Crocker

Design Firm: Crocker & Company, Hamilton MA **Client:** Boston University College of Engineering **Title:** 2002 Annual Report **Designer:** Peter Crocker

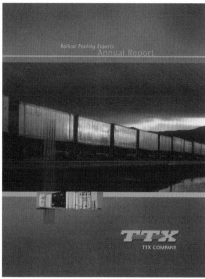

Design Firm: DeForest Creative, Elmhurst IL **Client:** TTX **Title:** Annual Report
Art Director: Wendy Weaver **Designer:** Wendy Weaver **Photographers:** Dick Dawson, Jim Panza, Tom Marion

Design Firm: Designwrite Advertising, Excelsior MN **Client:** Orphan Medical
Title: Annual Report **Designer:** Lisa Lenger

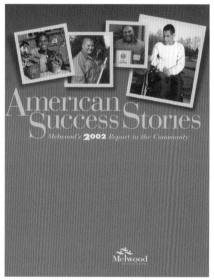

Design Firm: Dever Designs, Laurel MD **Client:** Melwood **Title:** Report to the Community **Art Director:** Jeffrey L. Dever **Designer:** Chris Komisar

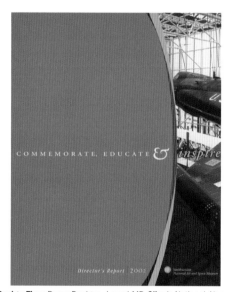

Design Firm: Dever Designs, Laurel MD **Client:** National Air and Space Museum **Title:** Director's Report **Art Director:** Jeffrey L. Dever **Designers:** Jeffrey L. Dever, Kristin Duffy

Design Firm: Emisphere Technologies, Inc., Tarrytown NY **Title:** Annual Report
Art Director: Stewart Siskind **Designer:** Stewart Siskind **Photographer:** Dan Lipow

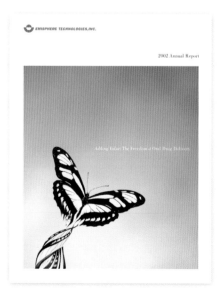

Design Firm: Emisphere Technologies, Inc., Tarrytown NY **Title:** Annual Report
Art Director: Stewart Siskind **Designer:** Stewart Siskind

Design Firm: Epstein Design Partners, Cleveland OH **Client:** Ulmer & Berne, LLP **Title:** Annual Report **Designer:** Karen Myers **Photographer:** Russell Lee

Design Firm: Ervin|Bell Advertising, Huntington Beach CA **Client:** The First American Corporation **Title:** Annual Report **Designer:** Jileen Hohle

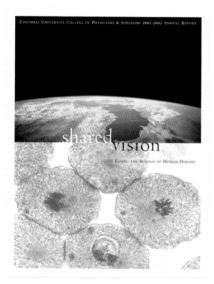

Design Firm: George/Gerard Design, New York NY **Client:** Columbia University College of Physicians & Surgeons **Title:** Shared Vision **Art Director:** Hershell George **Designer:** Hershell George **Photographer:** Robert Glick

Design Firm: Gomersall Design, Santa Barbara CA **Client:** Sheriff's Department - County of Santa Barbara **Title:** Sheriff's Annual Report **Art Director:** Dianne Gomersall **Designers:** Dianne Gomersall, Mimi Mowery **Photographers:** Lisa Hemman, Al Lafferty, Bernice Allen

Design Firm: Grange Insurance Companies, Columbus OH **Title:** Proud to Be Your Partner Annual Report **Art Director:** Chris Gosnell **Designer:** Dennis England **Photographers:** Dennis England, Jeff Rogers

Design Firm: Greenfield Belser Ltd., Washington DC **Client:** Helms Mulliss & Wicker **Title:** Annual Report **Art Director:** Burkey Belser **Designer:** Jon Bruns **Illustrator:** Tom Cameron

Design Firm: Griffith Phillips Creative, Dallas TX **Client:** Daisytek
Title: Annual Report **Designer:** Brian Niemann **Photographer:** Pete Lacker

Design Firm: Hare Strigenz Design, Milwaukee WI **Client:** Fresh Brands
Title: Annual Report **Art Director:** Paula Hare **Designer:** Emily Simonis

Design Firm: Hare Strigenz Design, Milwaukee WI **Client:** Weyco Group, Inc.
Title: Annual Report **Art Director:** Paula Hare **Designer:** Nicole Vogt

Design Firm: Hausman Design, Stanford CA **Client:** Ion Beam Applications
Title: Annual Report **Art Director:** Joan L. Hausman **Designer:** Joan L. Hausman
Photographer: Mark Tuschman

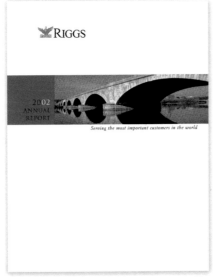

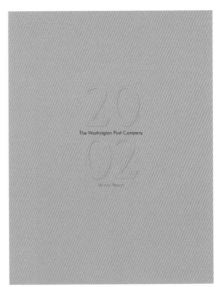

Design Firm: HC Creative Communications, Bethesda MD **Client:** Riggs
Bank **Title:** Annual Report **Art Directors:** Howard Clare, Jessica Vogel
Designer: Jessica Vogel

Design Firm: HC Creative Communications, Bethesda MD **Client:** The
Washington Post **Title:** Annual Report **Art Directors:** Howard Clare,
Jessica Vogel **Designer:** Jessica Vogel

Design Firm: HowellMartin Marketing & Advertising, Brattleboro VT
Client: FiberMark Title: Annual Report Art Director: Mel Martin Designer: Bill Jones
Illustrator: Brigette Soucy Photographer: Jim Gilmore

Design Firm: Ideas on Purpose, New York NY Client: Octel Corporation
Title: Annual Report Art Director: Darren Namaye Designer: Darren Namaye
Photographers: Paul Tozer and various

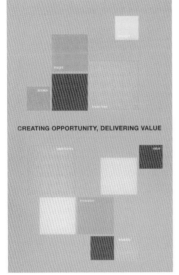

Design Firm: Ideas on Purpose, New York NY Client: NYCE Corporation
Title: Annual Review Art Director: John Connolly Designer: John Connolly
Illustrator: Sophie Blackall Photographer: Graham Haber

Design Firm: Ion Design, Frederick MD Client: St. James School Title: Annual
Report of Gifts Designer: Tom Gamerstsfelder Photographer: Historical

Design Firm: Lincoln Center for the Performing Arts, New York NY Title: Annual
Report Art Director: Peter J. Duffin Designer: Susan Siegrist Photographers: David
Lamb, Jane Hoffer, Steve Sherman, Susan Siegrist, Stephanie Berger

Design Firm: Nesnadny + Schwartz, Cleveland OH Client: The George
Gund Foundation Title: Annual Report Art Director: Mark Schwartz
Designer: Michelle Moehler Photographer: Barbara Bosworth

Design Firm: Nesnadny + Schwartz, Cleveland OH **Client:** The Eaton Corporation
Title: Annual Report **Art Directors:** Mark Schwartz, Greg Oznowich
Designers: Greg Oznowich, Teresa Snow **Photographer:** Design Photography

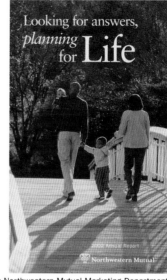

Design Firm: Northwestern Mutual Marketing Department, Milwaukee WI
Title: Looking for Answers, Planning for Life **Art Director:** Tommy Landis
Designer: Tommy Landis **Photographers:** Jim Peterson, Mike Miller

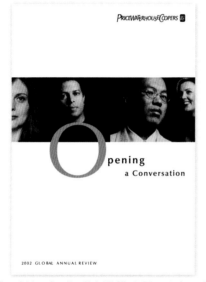

Design Firm: Odgis + Co., New York NY **Client:** PricewaterhouseCoopers
Title: Opening a Conversation **Art Director:** Janet Odgis **Designers:** Janet Odgis,
Wilfredo Cruz, Banu Berker

Design Firm: Paragraphs Design, Chicago IL **Client:** Coca-Cola FEMSA
Title: Annual Report **Art Director:** Meow Vatanatumrak
Designer: Meow Vatanatumrak **Photographer:** Todd Winters

Design Firm: Paragraphs Design, Chicago IL **Client:** IMC Global Inc.
Title: Annual Report **Art Directors:** Meow Vatanatumrak, Robin Zvonek
Designer: Meow Vatanatumrak **Photographers:** Greg Gillis and various

Design Firm: Paragraphs Design, Chicago IL **Client:** FEMSA
Title: Annual Report **Art Directors:** Jim Chilcutt, Rachel Radtke
Designer: Jim Chilcutt **Photographer:** Gabriel Covian

Design Firm: Paragraphs Design, Chicago IL **Client:** Exelon
Corporation **Title:** Annual Report **Art Directors:** Jim Chilcutt, Bonnie Simon
Designer: Jim Chilcutt **Photographer:** François Robert

Design Firm: Phoenix Creative Group, Herndon VA **Client:** ICI Mutual
Title: Annual Report **Art Director:** Nicole Kassolis **Designer:** Nicole Kassolis

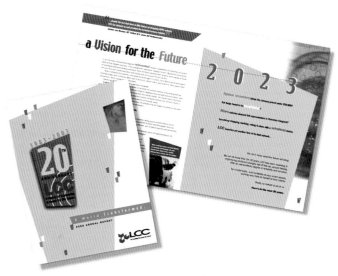

Design Firm: Phoenix Creative Group, Herndon VA **Client:** LCC International
Title: Annual Report **Art Director:** Nick Lutkins **Designer:** Angelo Buchanico
Illustrator: Angela Buchanico

Design Firm: Pite Creative, Superior CO **Client:** Ribozyme Pharmaceuticals
Title: Annual Report **Art Director:** Nicole Trousdale **Designer:** Johnathan Pite
Photographers: Michael Lichter, David Tejada

Design Firm: Plum Grove Printers, Hoffman Estates IL **Client:** Chicago Crime
Commission **Title:** Annual Report **Art Director:** Peter Lineal **Designers:** Katherine
Kirby, Linda Bond **Photographers:** Steven Becker, Bob Carl, Rita Kallman

Design Firm: Salomon Smith Barney , New York NY **Client:** Citigroup
Title: Citigroup Citizenship Report **Art Director:** Melita Sussman
Designer: Charles Miller

Design Firm: Sara Bernstein Design, Brooklyn NY **Client:** Bio-Technology General Corp. **Title:** Annual Report **Art Director:** Sara Bernstein **Designer:** Sara Bernstein **Photographer:** James Rudnick

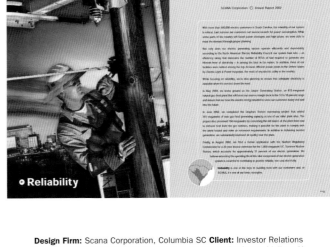

Design Firm: Scana Corporation, Columbia SC **Client:** Investor Relations **Title:** The Basics **Art Director:** Melissa H. Meadows **Designer:** Melissa H. Meadows **Photographer:** George Fulton

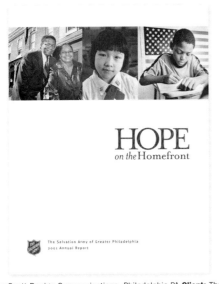

Design Firm: Scott Design Communications, Philadelphia PA **Client:** The Salvation Army of Greater Philadelphia **Title:** Annual Report **Art Directors:** Scott Feuer, Helene Krasney **Designer:** Phillip Go **Photographer:** Candace diCarlo

Design Firm: Stan Gellman Graphic Design, St. Louis MO **Client:** LaBarge Inc. **Title:** Annual Report **Art Director:** Barry Tilson **Designer:** Mike Donovan **Photographer:** Greg Kiger

Design Firm: studio/lab, Chicago IL **Client:** The Alzheimer's Association **Title:** Annual Report **Art Director:** Tara Kennedy **Designer:** Tara Kennedy **Photographer:** Angela Wyant

Design Firm: Tartan Marketing, Maple Grove MN **Client:** Antares Pharma **Title:** Annual Report **Designer:** Mike Dear **Writers:** Amy Rae Mason, Margie MacLachlan

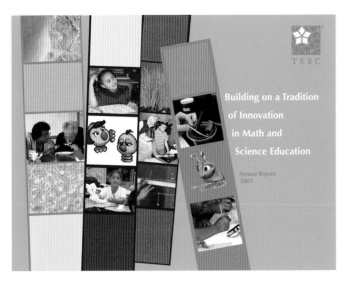

Design Firm: TERC, Cambridge MA **Title:** Annual Report
Art Director: Jane Sherrill **Designer:** Jane Sherrill

Design Firm: The College Board, New York NY **Title:** AP Yearbook
Designers: Reiner Designs, Kim Brown Irvis

Design Firm: The College of Saint Rose, Albany NY **Title:** Annual Report-
We have the power **Art Director:** Mark Hamilton **Designer:** Mark Hamilton
Photographers: Gary Gold, Luigi Benincasa

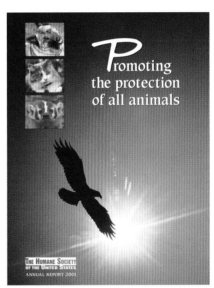

Design Firm: The Humane Society of the United States, Gaithersburg MD
Title: Promoting the Protection of All Animals **Art Director:** Paula Jaworski
Designer: Paula Jaworski

Design Firm: The Ideastudio LLC, Glastonbury CT **Client:** Bristol
Resource Recovery Facility Operating Committee **Title:** Annual Report
Art Director: John Mik **Designer:** John Mik

Design Firm: Thinkhouse Creative, Atlanta GA **Client:** Puget Energy
Title: Annual Report **Art Director:** Randy Allison **Designer:** Randy Allison
Photographer: Brian Sample

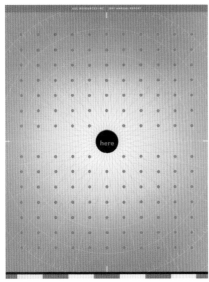

Design Firm: Thinkhouse Creative, Atlanta GA **Client:** AGL Resources
Title: Annual Report **Art Director:** Michael Matascik **Designer:** Michael
Matascik **Photographer:** Scott Lowden

Design Firm: Thinkhouse Creative, Atlanta GA **Client:** Georgia-Pacific
Title: Annual Review **Art Director:** Michael Matascik **Designer:** Michael Matascik
Photographer: Marc Norberg

Design Firm: UCSF University Publications & Public Affairs and IE Design +
Communication, Los Angeles CA **Client:** UCSF Comprehensive Cancer Center
Title: Annual Report **Art Director:** Carol Kummer, UCSF University Publications
& Public Affairs **Designer:** Marcie Carson, IE Design + Communication
Photographers: Majed & Kaz Tsuruta

Design Firm: UP Design LLC, Montclair NJ **Client:** Victoria Foundation
Title: Annual Report **Art Director:** Carin Manetti **Designer:** Gary Underhill

Design Firm: Yamamoto Moss, Minneapolis MN **Client:** Xcel Energy
Title: Annual Report **Art Director:** Joan Frenz **Designers:** Joan Frenz,
Amanda Baggenstoss **Photographer:** Joe Treleven

Design Firm: Zamboo, Marina Del Rey CA **Client:** Children's
Home Society of California **Title:** Reaching New Heights
Art Director: Dave Zambotti **Designer:** Jason Stillman

ADVERTISING

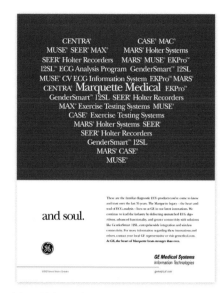

Design Firm: ArtSpace, Chester NY **Client:** Times Herald-Record **Title:** Record Of Your Life **Designer:** Mary T. Altobelli **Photographer:** Mary T. Altobelli

Design Firm: Avicom Marketing Communications, Waukesha WI **Client:** GE Medical Systems **Title:** Heart and Soul **Art Director:** Jeff McCulloch **Designer:** Jeff McCulloch

Design Firm: Avicom Marketing Communications, Waukesha WI **Client:** GE I-Sim **Title:** Superkid **Art Director:** Karyn Hadjinian **Designer:** Karyn Hadjinian

Design Firm: Big I Ranch Design Studio, Staten Island NY **Client:** Louisiana Office Of Tourism/Latina Magazine **Title:** Discover The Heart Of Spain **Art Director:** Irasema Rivera **Designer:** Irasema Rivera

Design Firm: Block Advertising & Marketing, Verona NJ **Client:** Medaglia D'Oro **Title:** Testimonial Ad Campaign **Art Director:** Karen DeLuca **Designer:** Jay Bauman

Design Firm: Cambridge Design Group, Andover MA **Client:** Orex Computed Radiography **Title:** International Product Ad **Art Director:** Rick Tracy **Designer:** Hernan Florez

Design Firm: Copeland Design, Potomac MD **Client:** EOS Financial Group
Title: Let's Face It **Art Director:** Ellen Copeland **Designer:** Stephen Macloud

Design Firm: Creative Fusion Design Company, Branford CT
Client: Notifier **Title:** Network Product Ad **Art Director:** Chris Walsh
Designers: Chris Walsh, Craig Des Roberts

Design Firm: Designwrite Advertising, Excelsior MN **Client:** TORO
Title: Scramble Sweepstakes **Designer:** Steve Siewert

Design Firm: DIRECTV, El Segundo CA **Client:** Internal Marketing Group
Title: PPV Movies 3-Page Spread **Creative Services Director:** Tiffany Iino
Senior Designer: Christi Lester **Design Manager:** Christine Pape

Design Firm: DIRECTV, El Segundo CA **Client:** Internal Marketing Group
Title: Freeview Print Ads **Creative Services Director:** Tiffany Iino
Senior Designer: Betsy Ullery **Design Manager:** Christine Pape

Design Firm: Division Street Design, Westlake OH **Client:** Westside
Automotive **Title:** Travel Journal Ad **Art Director:** Cynthia Peterson
Copywriter: Christine Lobas

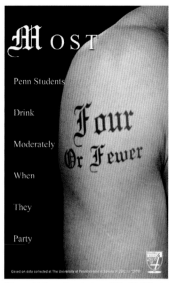

Design Firm: Drummond Design, Mayfield Heights OH Client: Snavely Development Company Title: The Preserve At Quail Hollow Campaign Art Director: Carol Drummond Designer: Carol Drummond Illustrator: Gary Kellner Photographer: Gary Kellner

Design Firm: Earthbound Interactive, Laguna Hills CA Client: The University of Pennsylvania Title: Alcohol Awareness Campaign Art Director: Blaine Behringer Designer: Brent Kreischer Photographer: Jesse Brossa

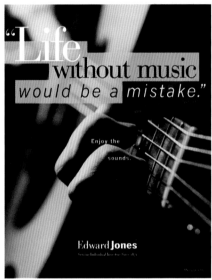

Design Firm: Edward Jones, St. Louis MO Client: Edward Jones Title: Jazz Festival Art Director: Brian Hopwood Designer: Holly Maddi

Design Firm: Edward Jones, St. Louis MO Client: Edward Jones Title: Above and Beyond Art Director: Brian Hopwood Designer: Jessica York

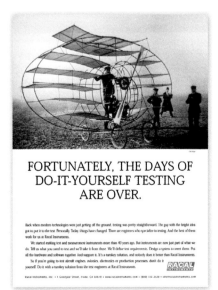

Design Firm: Flex Communication, Hauppauge NY Client: Racal Instruments, Inc. Art Director: Glenn Gemmell Designer: Glenn Gemmell

Design Firm: Flex Communication, Hauppauge NY Client: Racal Instruments, Inc. Art Director: Glenn Gemmell Designer: Glenn Gemmell

Design Firm: Flourish, Cleveland OH Client: The Designtex Group
Title: Birch Trees Art Director: Christopher Ferranti Designers: Steve Shuman,
Lisa Ferranti Photographer: Steve Shuman

Design Firm: Group One, Minneapolis MN Client: Parsinen Kaplan Rosberg & Gotlieb
P.A. Title: Estate Planning Art Director: Jennifer Meelberg Designer: Jennifer
Meelberg Illustrators: Bruce Weinberg, Melinda Nielsen Photographer: James Noble

Design Firm: Hickman + Associates, Indianapolis IN Client: Nevco
Scoreboard Company Title: Advertising Campaign Art Director: Chris Hansen
Designer: Chris Hansen

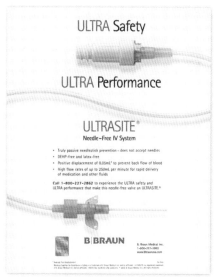

Design Firm: ImageSmith Advertising, Bridgewater NJ Client: B. Braun Medical
Title: ULTRASITE Full Page Ad Art Director: Candice Silva Designer: Richard Smith

Design Firm: International Paper, Memphis TN Client: International Paper Title:
Anniversary Poultry Ad Campaign Art Director: Roger Rasor Designer: Shea Morgan

Design Firm: Keck Garrett Associates, Chicago IL Client: Orange Glo International
Title: In The Dust Art Director: Cher Garrett Designer: Jim Bakasetas

Design Firm: Kelley Communications Group, Dublin OH **Client:** City of Dublin **Title:** City of Dublin Ads **Art Director:** Kevin Ronnebaum **Designers:** Betty Czekalski, Jamie Havens

Design Firm: Kendall Ross, Seattle WA **Client:** Bellevue Square **Title:** Ad Campaign **Art Director:** David Kendall **Designers:** David Kendall, Helen Kong **Photographers:** Zee Wendell, Jim Fagiolo

Design Firm: Kircher Inc., Washington DC **Client:** International Association of Amusement Parks and Attractions **Title:** Bigger Profits **Art Director:** Bruce E. Morgan **Designer:** Bruce E. Morgan **Photographer:** Tina Williams

Design Firm: Mary Jo Scibetta Design, Scottsdale AZ **Client:** Worldwide Licensing, The Coca-Cola Company **Title:** Popular Culture-Global Coverage **Creative Director:** Kelly Kozel (The Coca-Cola Company) **Art Director:** Mary Jo Scibetta

Design Firm: Novo Design Corporation, Red Bank NJ **Client:** Haven **Title:** Cuddle Chair **Art Director:** Ralph D. Finaldi **Designer:** Ralph D. Finaldi **Photographer:** David Van Scott

Design Firm: NYC Economic Development Corporation, New York NY **Title:** Apple Ad **Art Director:** Randi Press **Designer:** Matthew Shields

Design Firm: Open Eye Design, Fullerton CA **Client:** California Cove Communities Inc.
Title: The Crosby Advertisement **Art Director:** Fred Talactac **Designer:** Dan Haard

Design Firm: OrangeSeed Design, Minneapolis MN **Client:** Twin Cities Marathon
Title: Camera **Art Director:** Damien Wolf **Designers:** Damien Wolf, Phil Hoch
Photographer: Damien Wolf

Design Firm: Phoenix Creative Group, Herndon VA **Client:** Lafarge North America
Title: Cement Ad Series **Art Director:** Nick Lutkins **Designer:** Nicole Kassolis

Design Firm: Rvan Group, Plainville CT **Client:** Macton Corporation **Title:** Engineered
& Built to Last **Art Director:** Paul Klim **Designer:** Paul Klim **Illustrator:** Paul Klim

Design Firm: Sire Advertising, Lewisburg PA **Client:** Korogard Wall Protection
Systems **Title:** KWPG Ad **Art Director:** Shawn Felty **Designer:** Shawn Felty
Photographer: The Wild Studio

Design Firm: Sire Advertising, Lewisburg PA **Client:** Albright Care Services
Title: Surfing Ad **Designer:** Shawn Felty **Photographer:** Rob Trell

Design Firm: Talisman Interactive, Philadelphia PA **Client:** Zave Smith Photography
Title: Advertisement **Art Director:** Michael McDonald **Photographer:** Zave Smith

Design Firm: Templin Brink Design, San Francisco CA **Client:** Target Stores
Title: Michael Graves Advertising Campaign **Art Directors:** Joel Templin, Gaby Brink
Designer: Gaby Brink **Photographer:** David Campbell

Design Firm: Thinkhouse Creative, Atlanta GA **Client:** The Mohawk Group
Title: National Ad Campaign **Art Director:** Thinkhouse Creative
Designer: Thinkhouse Creative

Design Firm: Time Magazine/Time Marketing, New York NY **Client:** Scudder
Investments **Title:** Celebrating 75 Years of Time's Person of the Year
Art Director: Andrea Costa **Photographer:** Bill Eppridge

Design Firm: Tribune Media Services, Chicago IL **Client:** News in Motion
Title: News in Motion.com Ad Campaign **Art Director:** Oralia Anderson
Illustrators: Various **Photographers:** Various

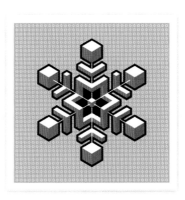

ANNOUNCEMENTS | INVITATIONS | CARDS

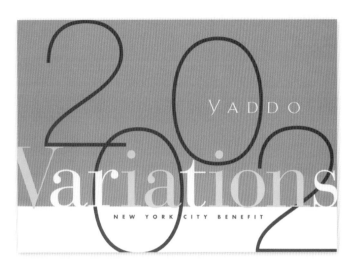

Design Firm: 2K Design, Clifton Park NY **Client:** Yaddo **Title:** Variations Invitation
Art Director: Kristine Fitzgerald **Designer:** Kristine Fitzgerald

Design Firm: Alberici Group, St. Louis MO **Client:** Alberci Constructors
Title: Detroit City Open House **Art Director:** Scott Tripp **Designer:** Scott Tripp

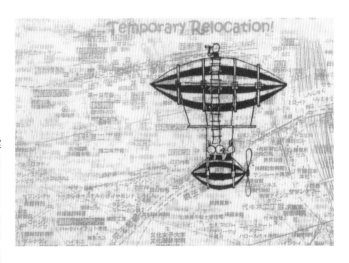

Design Firm: A&M Graphics, Los Altos CA **Client:** Trainor
Title: Moving Announcement **Designer:** Aleana Yiu

Design Firm: AM Creative, Chicago IL **Client:** Personal PAC
Title: Bastille Day Invitation **Designer:** Amy Masters

Design Firm: Artisa LLC, Plainsboro NJ **Client:** Princeton Symphony Orchestra
Title: Season Program Materials Campaign **Art Director:** Isabella D. Palowitch
Designer: Isabella D. Palowitch

Design Firm: Belyea, Seattle WA **Client:** ColorGraphics **Title:** Art Invitation Series
Art Director: Patricia Belyea **Designer:** Ron Lars Hansen

Design Firm: CAI Communications, Raleigh NC **Client:** Capital Associated Industries
Title: Habitat Invitation **Art Director:** Steve McCulloch **Designer:** Steve McCulloch

Design Firm: CAI Communications, Raleigh NC **Client:** North Carolina Dental Society
Title: Annual Session Mailer **Art Director:** Beth Greene **Designer:** Beth Greene

Design Firm: Children's Hospital of Pittsburgh, Pittsburgh PA **Client:** CHP Foundation
Title: A Night in the Outback **Designer:** Michael Tarquinio

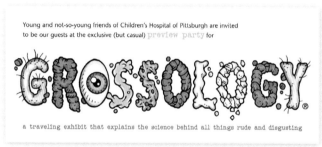

Design Firm: Children's Hospital of Pittsburgh, Pittsburgh PA **Client:** CHP Foundation
Title: Grossology Preview Party **Designer:** Kari Miller

Design Firm: Cisneros Design, Santa Fe NM **Client:** Buckaroo Ball
Title: Event Package **Art Director:** Brian Hurshman **Designer:** Yvette Jones
Illustrator: Timothy Jones

Design Firm: Cochran + Associates, Chicago IL **Client:** Bauhs Dring
Main Architects **Title:** Holiday Card **Art Director:** Bobbye Cochran
Designer: Bobbye Cochran **Illustrator:** Bobbye Cochran

Design Firm: Computer Associates International Inhouse Creative Development, Islandia NY **Client:** Computer Associates International **Title:** Corporate Holiday Card **Designer:** Malia Vrooman **Illustrator:** Malia Vrooman

Design Firm: Concentric Marketing, Charlotte NC **Client:** Open House Invite **Art Director:** Tricia Snead **Designer:** Sherry Williams **Photographer:** Jay Weinmiller **Copywriter:** Bob Shaw

Design Firm: Creative Dynamics Inc., Las Vegas NV **Client:** Caesars Palace, Las Vegas **Title:** A New Day: Celine Invite **Art Director:** Victor Rodriguez **Designer:** Mackenzie Walsh

Design Firm: Cull Design Group, Grand Rapids MI **Title:** Christmas Card **Art Director:** Scott Millen **Designer:** Scott Millen **Photographer:** Scott Millen

Design Firm: DCI Marketing, Milwaukee WI **Client:** Cadillac **Title:** Cadillac Color Cards **Art Director:** Tom Bruckbauer **Designer:** Tom Bruckbauer **Illustrator:** Bruce McNabb

Design Firm: Division Street Design, Westlake OH **Client:** Kellex Corporation **Title:** Postcard **Art Director:** Chris Clotz **Designer:** Christine Lobas **Illustrator:** Christine Lobas

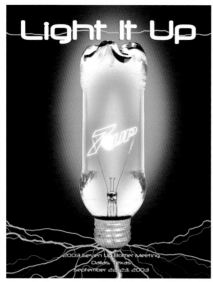

Design Firm: Dr. Pepper/Seven Worldwide, Plano TX **Title:** Light It Up
Invitation-Seven Up Bottler Meeting 2003 **Designer:** Brandon Adams

Design Firm: Earthlink, Pasadena CA **Title:** Holiday Party
Tickets **Art Director:** Vanina Cummings **Designer:** Scott Wong
Illustrators: Dan Sipple, Scott Wong

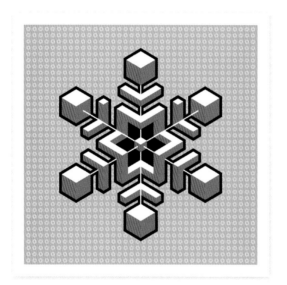

Design Firm: Flourish, Cleveland OH **Title:** Under The Microscope
Art Directors: Christopher Ferranti, Jing Lauengco **Designer:** Steve Shuman
Illustrator: Steve Shuman

Design Firm: Gee + Chung Design, San Franscisco CA **Client:** Applied Materials
Title: Seminar Invitations **Art Director:** Earl Gee **Designers:** Earl Gee, Fani Chung
Photographer: Kevin Ng

Design Firm: Hare Strigenz Design, Milwaukee WI **Client:** The Grace
Foundation **Title:** Chapeau Invitation **Art Director:** Juergen Strigenz
Designer: Emily Simonis

Design Firm: Heather Brady, Somerville MA **Clients:** Marissa Carli, Denise Fitzgerald,
Michelle Gorski **Title:** College Graduation Party Invite **Art Director:** Heather Brady
Designer: Heather Brady **Illustrator:** Heather Brady

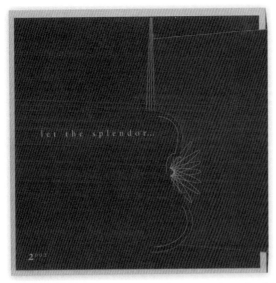

Design Firm: Hickman + Associates, Indianapolis IN Client: International Violin Competition Title: Invitation Art Director: Jenni Wilson Designer: Jenni Wilson

Design Firm: Hornall Anderson Design Works, Seattle WA Client: Erickson McGovern Title: Anniversary Promotional Piece Art Director: John Hornall Designers: John Hornall, Kathy Saito, Henry Yiu

Design Firm: House of Krauss, Columbus OH Client: German Village Society Title: Haus Und Garten Tour Invitation Art Director: Jason Krauss Designers: Jason Krauss, Jeremy Howell

Design Firm: IKON Communication & Marketing Design, Miami FL Client: Greater Miami Jewish Federation Title: Pillars of Pride Invitation Art Director: Randy Burman Designer: Randy Burman

Design Firm: Indysign Graphics, Minneapolis MN Client: Kevin Paulson & Callie Title: 2003 New Year's Eve Party Invite Art Director: Kevin Paulson Designer: Kevin Paulson Illustrator: Kevin Paulson

Design Firm: Innovative Advertising, LLC, Covington LA Client: Jay Blossman For Governor Title: Announcement Art Director: Amy Adams Hedgepath Designer: Amy Adams Hedgepeth Illustrator: Jay Connaughton Photographer: Jackson Hill

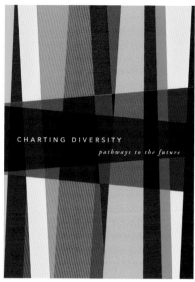

Design Firm: Ison Design, San Francisco CA **Client:** Legal Aid Society-Employment Law Center **Title:** Diversity Invitation **Designer:** Annabelle Ison

Design Firm: Ison Design, San Francisco CA **Client:** SF LGBT Center **Title:** Anniversary Invitation/Poster **Designer:** Annabelle Ison

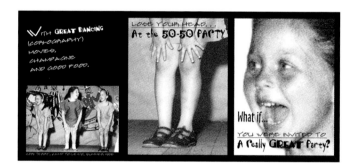

Design Firm: John Townsend Graphic Design, Kalamazoo MI **Client:** Wellspring/Cori Terry Dancers **Title:** Party Invitation **Designer:** John Townsend

Design Firm: Jones Design Group, Atlanta GA **Client:** Geographics **Title:** Open House Invitation **Art Director:** Vicky Jones **Designer:** Caroline McAlpine

Design Firm: KO11 Inc., East Brunswick NJ **Title:** Card **Art Director:** John Ko **Designers:** John Ko, Bran Bogdanovic **Illustrator:** John Ko

Design Firm: KRE8IVE Design, Cleveland OH **Client:** Greater Cleveland Growth Association **Title:** Public Officials Reception Invitation **Art Director:** Joseph S. Kovach **Designer:** Joseph S. Kovach

Design Firm: Los Alamos National Laboratory, Los Alamos NM
Client: Viz Team **Title:** Viz Postcard **Designer:** Allen Hopkins

Design Firm: Mid-Ohio Regional Planning, Columbus OH
Title: MORPC Annual Meeting Invitation and Program
Art Director: Marilyn Brown **Designer:** Edward Weding

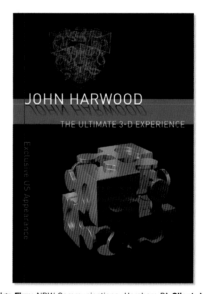

Design Firm: Million Dollar Round Table, Park Ridge IL **Title:** Top of the
Table Save the Date Cards **Designer:** Gabrielle R. Bowman

Design Firm: NDW Communications, Horsham PA **Client:** M-real
Title: John Harwood: Event Invitation **Art Director:** Bill Healey
Designer: Bill Healey **Illustrator:** John Harwood

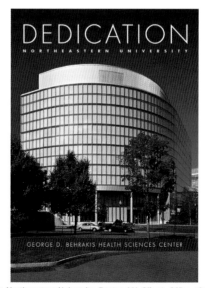

Design Firm: Northeastern University, Boston MA **Client:** Office of
Undergraduate Admissions **Title:** Prospectus **Art Director:** Mary Beth McSwigan
Designers: Jessica Schindhelm, Richard Pratt **Photographer:** Len Rubenstein

Design Firm: Northeastern University, Boston MA **Client:** Office of Advancement
Communications and Events **Title:** Behrakis Dedication Invite **Art Director:** Mary
Beth McSwigan **Designer:** Kelly Milligan **Photographer:** Len Rubenstein

Design Firm: Octavo Designs, Frederick MD **Client:** Enforme Interactive
Title: Holiday Card **Art Director:** Sue Hough **Designers:** Sue Hough,
Mark Burrier **Illustrator:** Mark Burrier

Design Firm: OrangeSeed Design, Minneapolis MN **Client:** Andersen Corporation
Title: Picture This **Art Director:** Damien Wolf **Designer:** Damien Wolf

Design Firm: Southern Company, Atlanta GA **Title:** Creating a Powerful Future
Art Director: Vicki Gardocki **Designer:** Kelli Stoudenmire Jones

Design Firm: Stan Gellman Graphic Design, St. Louis MO
Client: University of Illinois Foundation **Title:** Celebrating the Illinois Student
Art Director: Barry Tilson **Designer:** Mike Donovan

Design Firm: Stan Gellman Graphic Design, St. Louis MO
Client: University of Illinois Foundation **Title:** Spurlock Museum Dedication
Art Director: Barry Tilson **Designer:** Mike Donovan

Design Firm: Steffian Bradley Architects, Boston MA **Title:** 2003 Holiday Card
Art Director: Jackie Miller **Designer:** Jackie Miller

Design Firm: The Bancorp Bank, Wilmington DE **Title:** Cocktail Hour at Seattle Tradeshow **Art Director:** Amy Holt **Designer:** Amy Holt **Illustrator:** Amy Holt

Design Firm: The Bancorp Bank, Wilmington DE **Title:** Annual Party Invitation **Art Director:** Amy Holt **Designer:** Amy Holt

Design Firm: The Humane Society of the United States, Gaithersburg MD **Title:** Back to the Wild **Art Director:** Paula Jaworski **Designer:** Paula Jaworski

Design Firm: Wendy Miller Design, Chicago IL **Client:** Sue Duncan Children's Center **Title:** Evening of Fine Wine **Art Director:** Wendy M. Miller **Designer:** Wendy M. Miller **Illustrator:** Wendy M. Miller

Design Firm: ZGraphics, Ltd., East Dundee IL **Title:** Holiday Card **Art Director:** LouAnn Zeller **Designer:** Kris Martinez Farrell

BROCHURES AND COLLATERAL

Design Firm: 2K Design, Clifton Park NY Client: Albany Medical Center
Title: Biomedical Research Brochure Art Director: Kristine Fitzgerald
Designer: Kristine Fitzgerald Photographer: Mark McCarty

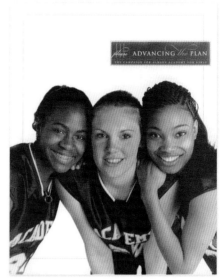

Design Firm: 2K Design, Clifton Park NY Client: Albany Academy
For Girls Title: Campaign Case Statement Art Director: Kristine Fitzgerald
Designer: Kristine Fitzgerald Photographer: Gary Gold

Design Firm: Aaron Design, New York NY Client: AIGA Title: Mentoring Brochure
Art Director: Stephanie Aaron Designer: Stephanie Aaron

Design Firm: American Music Group, Liverpool NY Client: American Music
Title: Step Up Brochure Art Director: Scott Herron Designer: Jason Anthony

Design Firm: AMS Users' Group, Irving TX Title: Conference
Program Designer: Randy Phelps

Design Firm: Anne Ink, Bloomfield Hills MI Client: Germack Pistachio Co.
Title: Retail Partnership Program Art Director: Anne Ink Designer: Anne Ink
Illustrator: Anne Ink Photographer: Anne Ink

Design Firm: Anne Ink, Bloomfield Hills MI **Client:** Door-Man Manufacturing
Title: Corporate Brochure **Art Director:** Anne Ink **Designer:** Anne Ink
Illustrator: Anne Ink **Photographer:** Anne Ink

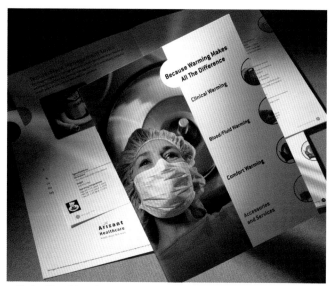

Design Firm: Arizant Healthcare Inhouse Design, Minneapolis MN **Client:** Arizant
Healthcare **Title:** Comprehensive Product Brochure **Art Director:** Mike Miller
Designer: Mike Miller **Photographer:** John Engstrom

Design Firm: Artenergy, Kentfield CA **Client:** H3R Inc. **Title:** Corporate
Brochure **Art Director:** Sergey Martinov **Designer:** Sergey Martinov

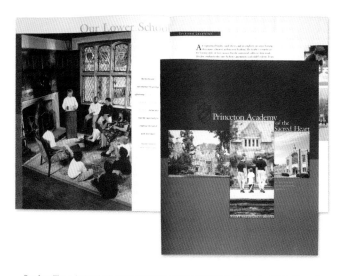

Design Firm: Artisa LLC, Plainsboro NJ **Client:** Princeton Academy of the Sacred
Heart **Title:** Princeton Academy Viewbook **Art Director:** Isabella D. Palowitch
Designer: Isabella D. Palowitch **Photographers:** Thomas Von Oehsen, Richard Speedy

Design Firm: Artisan/etalent, Chicago IL **Client:** Artisan/etalent **Title:** Corporate
Brochure **Art Director:** Michelle Holmes **Designer:** Michelle Holmes

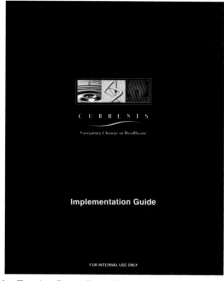

Design Firm: AstraZeneca Fusion Marketing Services, Wilmington DE
Title: Currents **Art Director:** Judy Frezza **Designer:** Judy Frezza

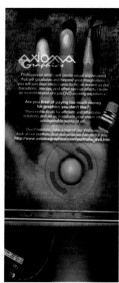

Design Firm: Austin Energy, Austin TX **Client:** Stephanie Phelps
Title: Emergency Outage Roladex **Art Director:** Stephanie Phelps
Designer: Stephanie Phelps **Photographer:** Juan Carrasco

Design Firm: Axioma Graphics, Lafayette CO **Title:** Brochure
Art Director: Irina Kiseleva **Designer:** Irina Kiseleva

Design Firm: Behan Communications, Glens Falls NY **Client:** D.A.
Collins Companies **Title:** Capabilities Brochure **Art Director:** Troy Burns
Designer: Troy Burns **Photographer:** Tom Grow

Design Firm: Behan Communications, Glens Falls NY **Client:** Finch Pruyn & Co.
Title: Finch Forestry **Art Director:** Troy Burns **Designer:** Troy Burns
Photographers: Tom Grow, Jerry Lemmo, Mike McMurray

Design Firm: Belyea, Seattle WA **Client:** K/P Corporation
Title: Brochure **Art Director:** Patricia Belyea **Designer:** Ron Lars Hansen
Photographer: Roseanne Olson

Design Firm: Black Graphics, San Francisco CA **Client:** The Highlands
Coalition **Title:** Vision Booklet **Art Director:** Karen Parry **Designer:** Karen Parry
Photographers: Various

Design Firm: Black Graphics, San Francisco CA **Client:** Eastern Forest Partnership **Title:** Vision Brochure **Art Director:** Karen Parry **Designer:** Karen Parry **Map:** Green Info Network **Photographers:** Various

Design Firm: Black Graphics, San Francisco CA **Client:** LawFund/NWSeed **Title:** Renewable Energy Atlas **Art Director:** Karen Parry **Designer:** Karen Parry **Map:** Green Info Network **Photographers:** Various

Design Firm: Blue Shield of California, San Francisco CA **Title:** Lifepath Advisers Member Brochure **Art Director:** Stephanie Donahue **Designer:** Olga Lopata

Design Firm: BMA Media Group, Cleveland OH **Title:** Juice Batteries Brochure **Art Director:** Ray Farrar **Designer:** Deb Mandley

Design Firm: Buck Consultants, St. Louis MO **Client:** Albertsons **Title:** today is your day **Art Director:** Stan Sams **Designer:** Elizabeth Lohmeyer

Design Firm: Buck Consultants, St. Louis MO **Client:** Albertsons **Title:** Store of the Year **Art Director:** Stan Sams **Designer:** Elizabeth Lohmeyer

Design Firm: Buck Consultants, St. Louis MO **Client:** Albertsons **Title:** Corus Volunteer Campaign **Art Director:** Stan Sams **Designer:** Elizabeth Lohmeyer

Design Firm: Buck Consultants, St. Louis MO **Client:** Fox Entertainment Group **Title:** Your 2003 Fox Employee Benefit Statement **Art Director:** Stan Sams **Designer:** Jennifer Sagaser **Photographer:** J. Baker (Ferguson & Katzman)

Design Firm: C&C Graphics, Malverne NY **Client:** TalkAids **Title:** TalkAids Promotional **Art Director:** Lisa L. Cangemi **Designer:** Lisa L. Cangemi

Design Firm: Cahan and Associates, San Francisco CA **Client:** Nektar Therapeutics **Title:** Nektar Supercritical Fluid Brochure **Art Directors:** Bill Cahan, Sharrie Brooks **Designer:** Sharrie Brooks **Illustrator:** Doug Struthers

Design Firm: Cahan and Associates, San Francisco CA **Client:** McKesson Corporation **Title:** Accordian-Fold Letter **Art Directors:** Bill Cahan, Sharrie Brooks **Designer:** Sharrie Brooks **Photographer:** Jeff Corwin

Design Firm: Cahan and Associates, San Francisco CA **Client:** McKesson Corporation **Title:** Corporate Brochure **Art Directors:** Bill Cahan, Sharrie Brooks **Designer:** Sharrie Brooks **Photographer:** Jeff Corwin

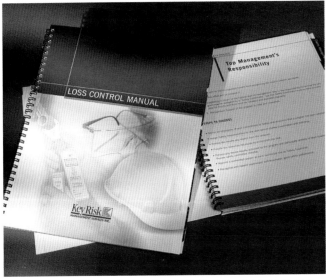

Design Firm: CAI Communications, Raleigh NC **Client:** Key Risk **Title:** Key Risk Loss Control Manual **Art Director:** Steve McCulloch **Designer:** Cathy Blair

Design Firm: CAI Communications, Raleigh NC **Client:** SoftPro Corporation **Title:** Brochure **Art Director:** Beth Greene **Designer:** Beth Greene **Illustrator:** Beth Greene

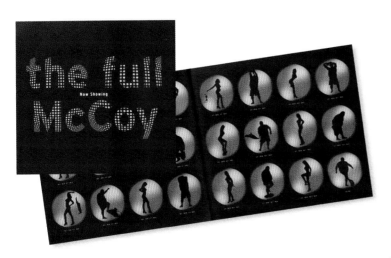

Design Firm: Carmichael Lynch Thorburn, Minneapolis MN **Client:** Potlatch **Title:** The Full McCoy **Creative Director:** Bill Thorburn **Designer:** David Schrimpf **Photographers:** Kevin Peterson, Neil Brown, Peter Carter

Design Firm: Cathereene Huynh Design, San Jose CA **Client:** Childrens' Creative Learning Centers **Title:** Corporate Overview Brochure **Art Director:** Cathe Huynh-Sison **Designer:** Cathe Huynh-Sison

Design Firm: CCBC, Baltimore MD **Title:** Smart Moves Brochure **Art Director:** Jodi Ceglia **Designer:** Jodi Ceglia

Design Firm: Charming Shoppes, Bensalem PA **Client:** Fashion Bug **Title:** Credit Card Program **Art Directors:** Steve McLerran, Lisbeth Harding **Designer:** Jennifer Sodorff

Design Firm: Chen Design Associates, San Francisco CA **Client:** Joe Goode
Performance Group **Title:** Mythic, Montana Campaign **Art Director:** Joshua C. Chen
Designers: Kathryn Hoffman, Joshua C. Chen **Photographer:** RJ Muna

Design Firm: Chen Design Associates, San Francisco CA **Client:** Sequoia Hospital
Title: Media Kit **Art Directors:** Joshua C. Chen, Kathryn Hoffman
Designers: Max Spector, Joshua Chen, Brian Singer **Photographer:** Jenny Thomas

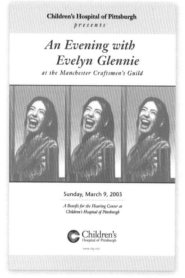

Design Firm: Children's Hospital of Pittsburgh, Pittsburgh PA
Client: CHP Foundation **Title:** An Evening with Evelyn Glennie
Art Director: Michael Tarquinio **Designer:** Jason Yurkovich

Design Firm: Christina Balas, Long Branch NJ **Client:** Morris Johnson & Associates
Title: Brochure/Collateral Materials **Designer:** Christina Balas

Design Firm: Cisneros Design, Santa Fe NM **Client:** Sharon McConnell
Title: Brochure **Art Director:** Brian Hurshman **Designer:** Brian Hurshman
Photographer: Eric Swanson

Design Firm: CMP Media LLC, Channel Group Design, Manhasset NY
Client: CRN **Title:** 2003 Media Kit **Art Director:** Brian A. McClean
Designer: Debra Cassa

Design Firm: CMP Media LLC,TSG Design, Manhasset NY Client: CMP XChange
Conferences Title: Event Kit Designer: Yoshide Hohokabe

Design Firm: Computer Associates International Inhouse Creative Development,
Islandia NY Client: Computer Associates International Title: Quality and Innovation
Brochure Art Director: Loren Moss Meyer Designer: Loren Moss Meyer

Design Firm: Crawford/Mikus Design, Atlanta GA Client: Elite Systems
Title: Capabilities Brochure Art Director: Elizabeth Crawford
Designer: Michelle May Photographers: Various

Design Firm: Crawford/Mikus Design, Atlanta GA Client: HCA Healthcare
Title: Enrollment Guide Art Director: Elizabeth Crawford Designer: Elizabeth
Crawford Illustrator: Laura Coyle

Design Firm: Crawford/Mikus Design, Atlanta GA Client: Standard Press
Title: Corporate Folder Art Director: Elizabeth Crawford
Designer: Elizabeth Crawford Photographers: Various

Design Firm: Crawford/Mikus Design, Atlanta GA Client: Wachovia
Title: Enrollment Materials Art Director: Elizabeth Crawford
Designer: Elizabeth Crawford Photographer: Various

Design Firm: Creative AIM, Southport CT **Client:** Pepsi **Title:** 2003 Diets Marketing Guide **Art Directors:** Tony D'Amico, Ann Lumpinski, Mark Barnes, Marc Phelan, Denise Arsenault **Designers:** Rich Phillips, James Ladner **Illustrator:** Oren Sherman

Design Firm: Creative Fusion Design Company, Branford CT **Client:** Davol **Title:** X-Stream Brochure **Art Director:** Craig Des Roberts **Designer:** Craig Des Roberts

Design Firm: Creative Fusion Design Company, Branford CT **Client:** License Monitor **Title:** Corporate Sales Brochure **Art Director:** Chris Walsh **Designer:** Chris Walsh

Design Firm: Creative Fusion Design Company, Branford CT **Client:** GE Corporate Financial Services **Title:** Corporate Marketing Kit **Art Director:** Craig Des Roberts **Designer:** Craig Des Roberts

Design Firm: Creative Fusion Design Company, Branford CT **Client:** GE Corporate Financial Services **Title:** Pocket Folder **Art Director:** Craig Des Roberts **Designer:** Craig Des Roberts

Design Firm: Cull Design Group, Grand Rapids MI **Client:** Old Orchard Brands **Title:** Retail Kit **Art Director:** Scott Millen **Designers:** Scott Millen, Allisa Hutchinson, Andy Meyer **Photographers:** Jim Powell, Chris Schnieter

Design Firm: Dan Rios Design, Davie FL **Client:** Greater Miami Visitor's Center
Title: Guest Directory **Art Director:** Dan Rios **Designer:** Dan Rios

Design Firm: DDB Worldwide, New York NY **Client:** NYC 2012
Title: If the Olympics Were Here **Art Director:** Mike Scheiner
Designer: Mike Scheiner **Photographer:** Kate Murphy

Design Firm: Del City, Milwaukee WI **Title:** New Product Announcements
Designer: Christine Hess

Design Firm: Dever Designs, Laurel MD **Client:** World Resources
Institute **Title:** WRI/TAI Folder **Art Director:** Jeffrey L. Dever
Designers: Jeffrey L. Dever, Kristin Duffy

Design Firm: Dever Designs, Laurel MD **Client:** Turn Key Office Solutions
Title: Turn Key Folder **Art Director:** Jeffrey L. Dever **Designer:** Jeffrey L. Dever

Design Firm: Diane Addesso Design, Worcester NY **Client:** Glimmerglass Opera
Title: Program Book **Art Director:** John Conklin **Designer:** Diane Addesso

Design Firm: Digital Frontier Group, Middle Island NY Client: City Outdoor
Title: Brochure Art Director: Vito Incorvaia Designer: Vito Incorvaia

Design Firm: DIRECTV, El Segundo CA Client: Internal Marketing Group
Title: HD POS Brochure Creative Services Director: Tiffany Iino
Senior Designer: Mollie Ritacco Design Manager: Louis Sanchez

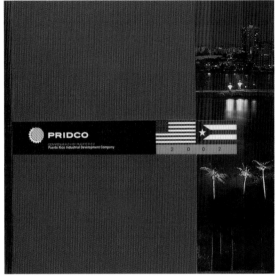

Design Firm: Edgar Omar Agosto, San Juan PR Client: Puerto Rico Industrial
Development Company Title: PRIDCO Brochure Art Director: Edgar Omar Agosto
Designer: Edgar Omar Agosto Illustrator: Edgar Omar Agosto
Photographers: Tomas Gual, Jorge Santana

Design Firm: Epstein Design Partners, Cleveland OH Client: Cuyahoga Community
College Title: Season Brochure Designer: Brian Jasinski Photographers: Various

Design Firm: Epstein Design Partners, Cleveland OH Client: Fairport Asset
Management Title: Annual Review Designer: Jileen Coy Photographer: Russell Lee

Design Firm: Evenson Design Group, Culver City CA Client: Mad Dogg Athletics
Title: Spinning Brochures Art Director: Stan Evenson Designer: Tricia Rauen

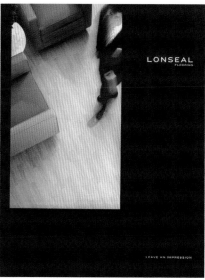

Design Firm: Ezzona Design Group, Burbank CA **Client:** Lonseal Flooring **Title:** Flooring Brochure **Art Directors:** James Pezzullo, Gina Vivona **Designer:** Nida Sanger **Illustrator:** Christopher Abando **Photographers:** Joshua White and Lonseal

Design Firm: FisherMears Associates, Liberty NY **Client:** The Woodstone Group **Title:** Chapin Estates Brochure **Designer:** Anne Dubrovsky

Design Firm: Franke + Fiorella, Minneapolis MN **Client:** 3M ESPE **Title:** RelyX Materials **Art Director:** Craig Franke **Designer:** Leslie McDougall **Illustrator:** Leslie McDougall **Photographer:** Joe Treleven Photography

Design Firm: G2 Worldwide, New York NY **Client:** The Absolut Spirits Company **Title:** Absolut Vanilia Trade Sample Kit **Art Director:** Michael Clarke **Designers:** Patrick Durgin-Bruce, Maria Samodra **Photographer:** Martin Wonnacott

Design Firm: Galperin Design Inc., New York NY **Client:** Temenos Villas **Title:** Temenos Brochure **Art Director:** Peter Galperin **Designer:** Peter Galperin **Photographers:** Elizabeth Zeschin, Andrew Spreitzer

Design Firm: Greenfield Belser Ltd., Washington DC **Client:** Cole Raywid & Braverman LLP **Title:** Brochure **Art Director:** Burkey Belser **Designer:** Tom Cameron **Illustrator:** Jon Bruns

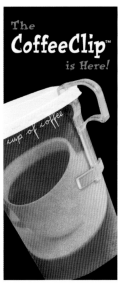

Design Firm: Gregory Richard Media Group, Pelham NY **Client:** Coffee Clip
Title: Brochure **Art Director:** Rich Sohanchyk **Designer:** Rich Sohanchyk

Design Firm: Gunn Design, Newton MA **Client:** Rowenta Inc.
Title: Product Brochures & Press Kits **Art Director:** Martha Heath
Designer: Martha Heath **Photographers:** David Shopper, Michael Indresano

Design Firm: Hanlon Brown Design, Portland OR **Client:** Willa Kenzie
Estate **Title:** Brochure **Art Director:** Sandy Brown **Designer:** Jon Schneider
Photographers: T.S. Whalen, Doreen L. Wynja

Design Firm: Hare Strigenz Design, Milwaukee WI **Client:** Florentine Opera
Title: Collateral Campaign **Art Director:** Juergen Strigenz **Designer:** Emily Simonis

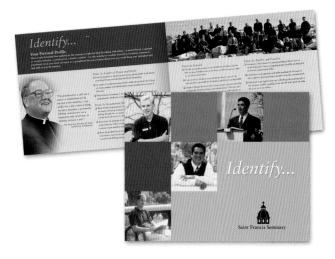

Design Firm: Hare Strigenz Design, Milwaukee WI **Client:** Saint Francis Seminary
Title: Recruiting Brochure **Art Director:** Paula Hare **Designer:** Holly Champagne

Design Firm: HC Creative Communications, Bethesda MD **Client:** CenterWorks
Title: Brochure **Art Directors:** Howard Clare, Jessica Vogel **Designer:** Jessica Vogel

Design Firm: HIDA (Health Industry Distributors Association), Alexandria VA
Title: HIDA Foundation Executive Conference Brochure **Designer:** Wendy Brewer

Design Firm: Highmark, Pittsburgh PA **Client:** PA Blue Shield **Title:** My Shield
Designer: Adam Isovitsch

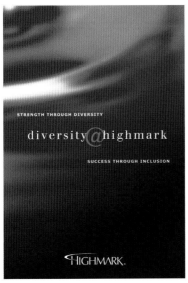

Design Firm: Highmark, Pittsburgh PA **Client:** Diversity Corporate
Workforce Initiatives **Title:** Diversity Website Promotion **Art Director:** Jay Hernishin
Designer: Jay Hernishin

Design Firm: Highmark, Pittsburgh PA **Client:** Highmark Life & Casualty
Title: National Sales Conference **Designer:** Melanie Young

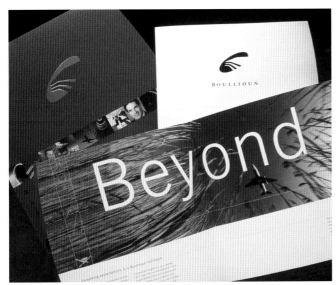

Design Firm: Hornall Anderson Design Works, Seattle WA **Client:** Boullion Aviation
Services **Title:** Coporate Brochure **Art Director:** Jack Anderson **Designers:** Katha
Dalton, Sonja Max, Henry Yiu, Hillary Radbill, Micheal Brugman

Design Firm: Hornall Anderson Design Works, Seattle WA **Client:** Orivo **Title:** Orivo
Brochure **Art Director:** Jack Anderson **Designers:** Jack Anderson, Andrew Wicklund,
Henry Yiu **Photographers:** Andrew Wicklund and various

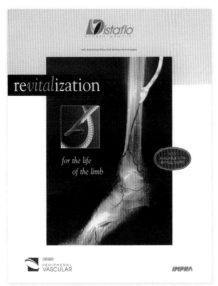

Design Firm: ImageSmith Advertising, Bridgewater NJ **Client:** Bard
Peripheral Vascular **Title:** Distaflo Brochure **Art Director:** Candice Silva
Designer: Candice Silva

Design Firm: Innovative Advertising, LLC, Covington LA **Client:** Franco's Athletic Club
Title: Brochure **Creative Director:** Jay Connaughton **Art Director:** Elizabeth Guidry
Badeaux **Designer:** Elizabeth Guidry Badeaux

Design Firm: Inova Health System, Springfield VA **Client:** Life With Cancer
Title: Kit Folder and Inserts **Art Director:** Rachel Arnold **Designer:** Vizuäl, Inc.
Illustrator: Wilmot Sanz

Design Firm: Inova Health System, Springfield VA **Title:** Not-For-Profit Brochure
Art Director: Jayne Catullo **Designer:** Catalyst Design

Design Firm: InteloQuence, Greneva IL **Title:** If You Don't See It You
Don't Get It **Art Director:** Dan Elliott **Designer:** Dan Elliott **Illustrator:** Dan Elliott
Photographer: Dan Elliott

Design Firm: Interactive Network for Continuing Education (INCE), Cranbury NJ
Client: GlaxoSmithKline **Title:** Diabetes Directing Patient Care **Art Director:** Jamie
Santiago **Designers:** Jamie Santiago, Tracy Sullivan, Kim Silverman

Design Firm: International Paper, Memphis TN **Title:** Product Sales Sheets
Art Director: Roger Rasor **Designers:** Shea Morgan, Terry Jarred

Design Firm: International Paper, Memphis TN **Title:** Bulk Packaging Food Brochure
Art Director: Roger Rasor **Designer:** Shea Morgan **Illustrator:** Shea Morgan

Design Firm: Ion Design, Frederick MD **Client:** National Recreation &
Park Association **Title:** July Is Recreation & Parks Month **Art Director:** Ruth
Bielobocky **Designer:** Eryn Willard

Design Firm: Island Oasis, Walpole MA **Client:** Island Oasis Frozen Beverage Co.
Title: Rave Martini Brochure **Designer:** Peter Buhler **Photographer:** Peter Buhler

Design Firm: Island Oasis, Walpole MA **Client:** Island Oasis
Frozen Beverage Co. **Title:** Brochure **Art Director:** Ian Shippard
Designer: Ian Shippard **Photographer:** Peter Buhler

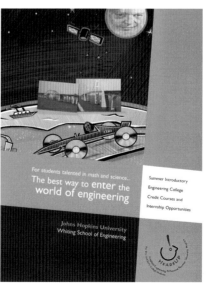

Design Firm: Jill Tanenbaum Graphic Design & Advertising, Bethesda MD
Client: John Hopkins University **Title:** Heads Up **Art Director:** Jill Tanenbaum
Designer: Sue Sprinkle **Illustrator:** Tom Garrett

Design Firm: Jones Design Group, Atlanta GA **Client:** Coca-Cola
Title: Implementation Manual **Art Director:** Vicky Jones **Designer:** Betsy Perez

Design Firm: Kaleidoscope Design, Snohomish WA **Client:** Seco Development
Title: Chelsea at Juanita Village Brochure **Art Director:** Cynthia Lynn
Designer: Cynthia Lynn **Illustrator:** Robert Williamson

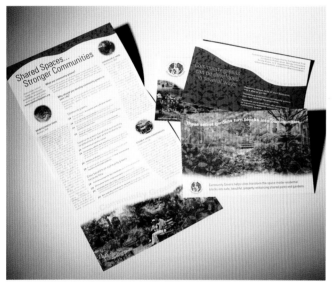

Design Firm: Kittner Design, Takoma Park MD **Client:** Community Greens
Title: Fundraising Brochure **Art Director:** Bobbi Kittner **Designers:** Bobbi Kittner,
Karen O'Hara, Kristin Kaineg

Design Firm: Kittner Design, Takoma Park MD **Client:** TomPaine.com
Title: Corporate Brochure **Art Director:** Bobbi Kittner **Designers:** Bobbi
Kittner, Karen O'Hara

Design Firm: KRE8IVE Design, Cleveland OH **Client:** TMW Systems
Title: 20th Anniversary Brochure **Art Director:** Joseph S. Kovach
Designer: Joseph S. Kovach

Design Firm: Laurel Black Design, Port Angeles WA **Client:** City of Port Angeles/
Clallam County EDC **Title:** Port Angeles Works Business Recruitment
Brochure **Art Director:** Laurel Black **Designer:** Laurel Black Design
Photographers: Greg Thon, Rich Riski

Design Firm: Lentini Design, Los Angeles CA **Title:** LACC Marketing Collateral
Art Director: Hilary Lentini **Designer:** Hilary Lentini

Design Firm: Lincoln Center for the Performing Arts, New York NY **Title:** Lincoln Center Festival Brochure **Art Director:** Peter J. Duffin **Designer:** Stephanie Coleman-Simon **Photographers:** Nan Keeton, Judy McEvoy, Stephanie Simon

Design Firm: Logistics Management Institute, McClean VA **Title:** LMI Capabilities Brochure **Art Directors:** Kathy Myers, Barbara Taff **Designer:** Barbara Taff **Illustrator:** Brian Jensen **Photographer:** Jim Douglas

Design Firm: Los Alamos National Laboratory, Los Alamos NM **Client:** Environmental Restoration Group **Title:** Citizens Guide and Folder **Art Director:** Kelly L. Parker **Designer:** Kelly L. Parker

Design Firm: Marriott Vacation Club International, Orlando FL **Title:** Recruitment Brochure **Art Director:** Allison Schwartz **Designer:** Allison Schwartz **Photographers:** Various

Design Firm: Marriott Vacation Club International, Orlando FL **Title:** Recruitment Brochure **Art Director:** Chrissy Selesky **Designer:** Chrissy Selesky **Photographers:** Various

Design Firm: Martini Design, Shelton CT Client: Greater Bridgeport Transit Authority Title: Initiatives Presentation Folder Art Director: Susan Martini Designer: Susan Martini

Design Firm: Mira Design Studio, Atlanta GA Client: The Arthur M. Blank Family Foundation/Trillium Consulting Title: Grantee Conference Collateral Art Director: Renée Boncore Designer: Renée Boncore Photographer: Ilene Perlman

Design Firm: Moonshadow Design, Greenville NH Client: Desktop Engineering Magazine Title: Media Kit Designer: April Walker

Design Firm: Moonshadow Design, Greenville NH Client: Supply Chain System Magazine Title: Media Kit Designer: April Walker

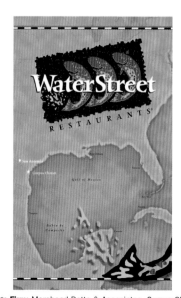

Design Firm: Morehead Dotts & Associates, Corpus Christi TX Client: WaterStreet Restaurant Title: Menu Designer: Janet Wilems

Design Firm: NDW Communications, Horsham PA Client: Fox River Paper Title: Sundance: On the Job (Issue 2) Art Director: Tom Brill Designer: Tom Brill Photographer: Dan Naylor

Design Firm: NDW Communications, Horsham PA **Client:** M-real **Title:** United By Design **Art Director:** Bill Healey **Designer:** Bill Healey **Photographer:** Dan Naylor

Design Firm: New Jersey Housing and Mortgage Finance Agency, Trenton NJ **Title:** Smart Growth Action Kit **Art Director:** Ana Maria Rivera-Pramuk **Designer:** Ana Maria Rivera-Pramuk

Design Firm: New Jersey Housing and Mortgage Finance Agency, Trenton NJ **Title:** Housing Conference Registration **Art Director:** Ana Maria Rivera-Pramuk **Designer:** Ana Maria Rivera-Pramuk

Design Firm: NHL Creative Services, New York NY **Client:** NHL Events & Entertainment **Title:** All-Star Invitation Package **Art Directors:** Paul Conway, Kathy Drew **Designer:** Paul Conway

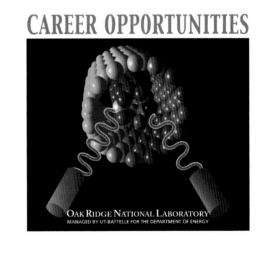

Design Firm: NYC Economic Development Corporation, New York NY **Title:** Liberty Bond **Art Director:** Randi Press **Designer:** Matthew Shields

Design Firm: Oak Ridge National Laboratory/UT-Battelle, Oakridge TN **Client:** Human Resources **Title:** Career Opportunities **Art Director:** Peggy Brown **Designer:** Vickie L. Conner **Photographers:** Curtis Boles, Jim Richmond

Design Firm: Octavo Designs, Frederick MD Client: National Association of School Psychologists Title: School Psychology Brochure Art Director: Sue Hough Designers: Octavo Team

Design Firm: Open Eye Design, Fullerton CA Client: Genera Corporation TYC Title: Elegante Product Brochure Trucks Art Director: Fred Talactac Designer: Grace Lozano Photographer: Fred Talactac

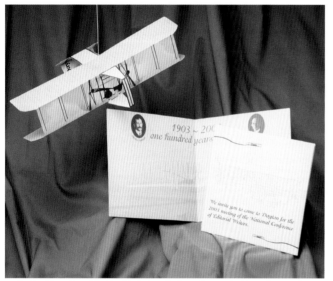

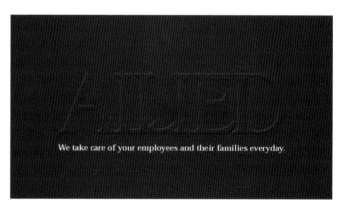

Design Firm: Out of the Box Marketing, Hoffman Estates IL Client: Daytona Daily News Title: Brochure Designer: Brad Pencil

Design Firm: Out of the Box Marketing, Hoffman Estates IL Client: Allied Benefits Title: Brochure Designer: Brad Pencil

Design Firm: Page Design Inc., Sacramento CA Client: Dome Printing Title: Dome Baby Brochure Art Director: Paul Page Designer: Chris Brown Illustrators: Kurt Kland, Sherril Cortez Photographer: Donald Satterlee

Design Firm: Pearson Learning Group, Parsippany NJ Title: Using Primary Sources Overview Art Director: Linda Hoffman Designer: Angel Devost, Devost Design Photographers: Various

Design Firm: Pearson Learning Group, Parsippany NJ **Title:** Concepts and Challenges Overview **Art Director:** Linda Hoffman **Designer:** Angel Devost, Devost Design **Photographers:** Various

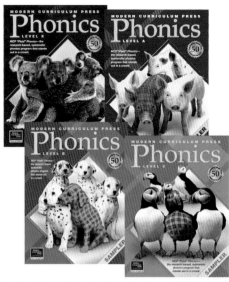

Design Firm: Pearson Learning Group, Parsippany NJ **Title:** MCP Plaid Phonics Samplers **Art Director:** Linda Hoffman **Designer:** Kristin Rider **Photographer:** Karen Mancinelli

Design Firm: Pearson Learning Group, Parsippany NJ **Title:** Pacemaker Series **Art Director:** Linda Hoffman **Designer:** Kristin Rider **Photographers:** Various

Design Firm: Pearson Learning Group, Parsippany NJ **Title:** Pacemaker Biology Sampler **Art Director:** Linda Hoffman **Designer:** Angel Devost, Devost Design **Photographers:** Various

Design Firm: Pikala Design Company, Minneapolis MN **Client:** William Mitchell College of Law **Title:** A Foundation for the Future **Art Director:** Steve Pikala **Designer:** Steve Pikala **Photographers:** Various

Design Firm: Pite Creative, Superior CO **Client:** International ShipRecycling Limited **Title:** Brochure **Designer:** Jonathan Pite

Design Firm: PreV ision, Lincoln MA **Client:** Stride Rite **Title:** New Moms Welcome Kit **Art Directors:** Michael Chrisner, George Lepore **Designers:** Floyd Sipe, Carla Arriaga **Illustrator:** Emilie Chollat **Photographer:** Ross Whitaker **Writer:** Diana Kirk

Design Firm: Project 03, North Aurora IL **Client:** Comprehensive Rehab Inc. **Title:** Company Brochure **Designer:** Project 03

Design Firm: Rappy & Company, New York NY **Client:** Girl Scouts of the USA **Title:** Studio 2B Marketing Kit **Art Director:** Floyd Rappy **Designers:** Floyd Rappy, Jose San Juan **Photographer:** Bill Milne

Design Firm: Rappy & Company Inc., New York NY **Client:** eBay **Title:** eBay-Sell...Splurge...Repeat! **Art Director:** Floyd Rappy **Designers:** Floyd Rappy, Jose San Juan **Photographer:** Bill Milne

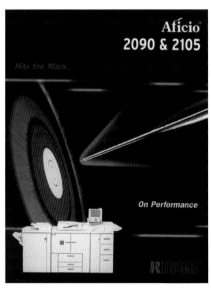

Design Firm: Ricoh Corporation, West Caldwell NJ **Title:** You Are What You Produce **Art Directors:** Wendy Helft, Ron Mowrey, Cliff Campbell **Designer:** UP Design LLC **Photographer:** New Era Studio

Design Firm: Ricoh Corporation, West Caldwell NJ **Client:** Production Systems Marketing of Ricoh **Title:** Aficio 2090 & 2105 **Art Directors:** Elisa E. Esposito, Linda Montefusco **Designer:** Elisa E. Esposito **Photographer:** F90

Design Firm: Rule29, Elgin IL **Client:** O'Neil Printing **Title:** Brochure
Art Directors: Justin Ahrens, Jim Bobori **Designers:** Justin Ahrens, Jim Bobori
Photographer: Brian MacDonald

Design Firm: Rutgers, The State University of New Jersey, New Brunswick NJ
Client: New Jersey EcoComplex **Title:** New Jersey EcoComplex Brochure
Art Director: John Van Cleaf **Designer:** John Van Cleaf **Photographers:** Alan
Goldsmith, Nick Romanenko

Design Firm: Rutgers, The State University of New Jersey, New Brunswick NJ
Client: Zimmerl Art Museum **Title:** Sergei Parajanov Catalog
Art Director: Gerald D. Meccia **Designer:** Gerald D. Meccia

Design Firm: Rutgers, The State University of New Jersey, New Brunswick NJ
Client: Rutgers Business School **Title:** Rutgers Business School Package
Art Director: John Van Cleaf **Designer:** Sean Tarricone

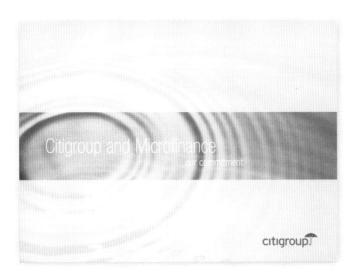

Design Firm: Salomon Smith Barney, New York NY **Client:** Citigroup Foundation
Title: Citigroup & Microfinance **Creative Director:** Melita Sussman
Art Director: Frank Gitro **Designer:** Frank Gitro

Design Firm: Salomon Smith Barney, New York NY **Client:** Citigroup
Global Prime Brokerage **Title:** Prime Broker Brochure **Art Director:** Melita Sussman
Designer: Carla Magazino

Design Firm: Salomon Smith Barney, New York NY **Client:** Global Recruiting **Title:** This is Citigroup **Creative Director:** Melita Sussman **Art Director:** Frank Gitro **Designer:** Frank Gitro **Photographer:** Jonathan Torgovnik

Design Firm: Salomon Smith Barney, New York NY **Client:** Salomon Smith Barney Lending Services **Title:** Credit Lending Capabilities **Art Director:** Melita Sussman **Designer:** Carla Magazino

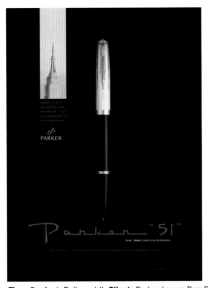

Design Firm: Sanford, Bellwood IL **Client:** Parker Luxury Pen Division **Title:** Parker 51 Limited Edition **Art Director:** Cari Salpaka Owen **Designer:** Lucy Biancofiore

Design Firm: Scott Design Communications, Philadelphia PA **Client:** ARAMARK Healthcare Support Services **Title:** HSS Kit **Art Directors:** Scott Feuer, Helene Krasney **Designers:** Audrey Ziegler, Jeanine Testa

Design Firm: Shelby Design & Illustrates, Oakland CA **Client:** Maritz Inc./ Ariba Inc. **Title:** Ariba Live Conference Guide **Art Director:** Shelby Putnum Tupper **Designer:** Molly McCoy

Design Firm: Sherman Advertising, New York NY **Client:** Roseland Properties **Title:** The Brownstones Brochure **Art Director:** Diana Wheaton **Designer:** Sharon Lloyd McLaughlin **Illustrator:** James Akers

Design Firm: Simple Design, Golden CO **Client:** Boston Market
Title: Catering Brochure **Art Director:** Robert Mitchell **Designer:** Greg Marko
Illustrator: Jason Stalker **Photographer:** DeGennaro

Design Firm: Sire Advertising, Lewisburg PA **Client:** Brodart Company
Title: Metro Chair **Art Director:** Shawn Felty **Designer:** Shawn Felty
Photographer: The Wild Studio

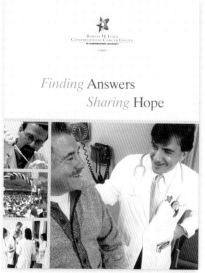

Design Firm: Stan Gellman Graphic Design, St. Louis MO **Client:** Robert H. Lurie
Comprehensive Cancer Center **Title:** Finding Answers Sharing Hope
Art Director: Barry Tilson **Designer:** Mike Donovan

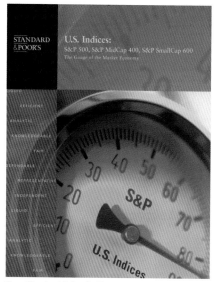

Design Firm: Standard & Poor's Financial Communications, Boston MA
Client: Standard & Poor's Index Services **Title:** Hong Kong Indices
Creative Director: Kathleen Austin **Design Manager:** Greg Galvan
Photographer: Jim Barber

Design Firm: Tartan Marketing, Maple Grove MN **Client:** HR Simplified
Title: Brochure **Designer:** Barry McCullough **Illustrator:** Beth Hatlen
Writer: Amy Rae Mason

Design Firm: Tartan Marketing, Maple Grove MN **Client:** Land O'Lakes Ingredient
Solutions **Title:** Capabilities Brochure **Designer:** Kim Werter
Writer: Margie MacLachlan

Design Firm: The Bancorp Bank, Wilmington DE **Title:** Business Banking Booklet
Art Director: Amy Holt **Designer:** Amy Holt

Design Firm: The College of Saint Rose, Albany NY **Title:** Campus Toolkit
Art Director: Mark Hamilton **Designer:** Mark Hamilton **Illustrator:** Chris Parody

Design Firm: The Humane Society of the United States, Gaithersburg MD
Title: A Safe Cat Is A Happy Cat **Art Director:** Paula Jaworski **Designer:** Paula Jaworski

Design Firm: The Humane Society of the United States, Gaithersburg MD
Title: Protecting Wildlife **Art Director:** Paula Jaworski **Designer:** Paula Jaworski

Design Firm: The Humane Society of the United States, Gaithersburg MD
Title: A Safe Cat is a Happy Cat (Package) **Art Director:** Paula Jaworski
Designer: Paula Jaworski

Design Firm: The Nelson-Atkins Museum Of Art, Kansas City MO **Title:** Business
Council Membership Packet **Art Director:** Molly Alspaugh **Designer:** Molly Alspaugh
Photographers: Rob Newcombe, Jamison MIller

Design Firm: The Shamrock Companies, Westlake OH **Client:** Watt Printers
Title: Capability Brochures **Art Directors:** Dave Larson, John Bennett
Designer: Lori Leiter **Illustrator:** Artists Studios

Design Firm: Thinkhouse Creative, Atlanta GA **Client:** The Coca-Cola Company
Title: Redefining Convenience **Art Director:** Thinkhouse Creative **Designer:**
Thinkhouse Creative **Illustrator:** Thinkhouse Creative

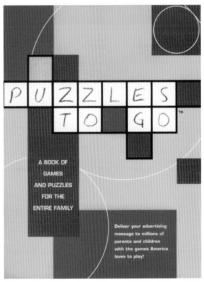

Design Firm: Tribune Media Services, Chicago IL **Client:** News & Features/TMS
Title: Joe Martin Folder **Designer:** Matt Maldre **Illustrator:** Joe Martin

Design Firm: Tribune Media Services, Chicago IL **Client:** News & Features/TMS
Title: Puzzles To Go Folder **Designer:** Stephani Kuehn

Design Firm: Tribune Media Services, Chicago IL **Client:** News & Features/TMS
Title: House Broken Folder **Designer:** Stephani Kuehn **Illustrator:** Steve Watkins

Design Firm: Tribune Media Services, Chicago IL **Client:** VUE **Title:** OverVUE Booklet
Art Director: Jill Sherman **Photographers:** Various

Design Firm: U.S. General Accounting Office, Washington DC **Client:** GAO
Title: Security, Take it Personally **Designer:** Jena Sinkfield

Design Firm: Uncommon Design, Laurel MD **Client:** QX Medpro Inc.
Title: QX Medpro Kit Folder **Art Director:** Carla Conway **Designer:** Carla Conway

Design Firm: Verizon Multimedia, Arlington VA **Client:** Verizon Human
Resources **Title:** Diversity Print Collateral **Art Director:** Debbie DeLadurantaye
Designer: Debbie DeLadurantaye

Design Firm: Verizon Multimedia, Arlington VA **Client:** Verizon Communications
Title: Progress Leaders Welcome Kit **Creative Director:** Patrik Wager **Art Director:**
Davie Smith **Designers:** Davie Smith, Davia Lilly **Illustrator:** Charles Yoakum

Design Firm: Western Interstate Commission for Higher Education (WICHE),
Boulder CO **Title:** Annual Meeting Preliminary Program **Art Director:** Candy Allen
Designer: Candy Allen **Illustrator:** Candy Allen **Photographer:** Candy Allen

Design Firm: WestGroup Communication, New York NY **Client:** Gloria Bass Design
Title: Stacking Rings-Brochure **Art Director:** Marvin Berk **Designer:** Marvin Berk

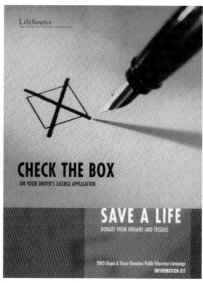

Design Firm: Yamamoto Moss, Minneapolis MN Client: LifeSource Title: Driver's License Campaign Kit Art Director: Miranda Kennedy Designers: Miranda Kennedy, Amanda Baggenstoss, Jane Calvin Photographer: Ellie Kingsburg

Design Firm: Yamamoto Moss, Minneapolis MN Client: Island Cruises Title: Island Cruises Brochure Art Director: Scott Miller Designer: Miranda Kennedy

Design Firm: Zamboo, Marina Del Rey CA Client: Nossaman Title: Corporate Folder Art Director: Dave Zambotti Designer: Colleen Parks

Design Firm: Zamboo, Marina Del Rey CA Client: UCI Medical Center Title: Aesthetic Center Art Director: Dave Zambotti Designer: Colleen Parks

Design Firm: Zamboo, Marina Del Rey CA Client: Cox Castle Nicholson Title: Forward Art Director: Becca Bootes Designer: Colleen Parks

Design Firm: ZGraphics, Ltd., East Dundee IL Client: Kenny Construction Power Group Title: Capabilities Brochure Art Director: Joe Zeller Designer: Renee Clark

Nov.03

the james beard foundation

calendar

THE 2003 JAMES BEARD FOUNDATION HOLIDAY AUCTION RAFFLE

CALENDARS

Design Firm: Computer Associates International Inhouse Creative
Development, Islandia NY Title: Computer Associates Corporate Calendar
Art Director: Jennifer Mariotti Williams Designer: Kristi M. Latuso

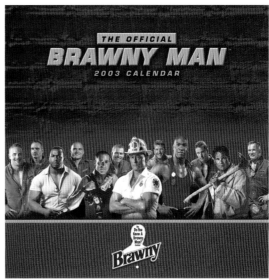

Design Firm: DVC Worldwide, Morristown NJ Client: Georgia-Pacific
Title: Do You Know a Brawny Man? Art Directors: Jeff Rubin, Tony Siminerio
Photographer: Allan Shoemake

Design Firm: Fluxhaus Design, New York NY Client: The James Beard Foundation
Title: Calendar/Previews Art Director: Scott Meola Designer: Scott Meola

Design Firm: Ginkgo Creative, Chicago IL Client: Munro Campagna Title: Chicago
Shakespeare Theater Calendar Art Director: Gina Luoma
Designers: Gina Luoma, Katie Rundell Illustrators: Various Photographer: Dimitre

Design Firm: Kensington Creative Worldwide, Inc., McLean VA Client: Exxon Mobil
Title: Marine Lubricants Calendar Designer: Jon Saunders

Design Firm: Kensington Creative Worldwide, Inc., McLean VA
Client: Kensington Creative Worldwide, Inc. Title: Calendar

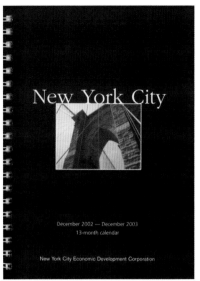

Design Firm: NYC Economic Development Corporation, New York NY
Title: Datebook **Art Director:** Randi Press **Designer:** Randi Press

Design Firm: Stan Gellman Graphic Design, St. Louis MO
Client: Marubeni Pulp & Paper North America **Title:** Topkote 2003
Art Director: Teresa Thompson **Designer:** Jill Lampen

Design Firm: Woman's Day Creative Services, New York NY **Title:** Woman's Day
Editorial Calendar **Art Director:** Beth Ann Silvestri **Designer:** Beth Ann Silvestri
Photographers: Various

DIRECT MAIL AND DIRECT RESPONSE

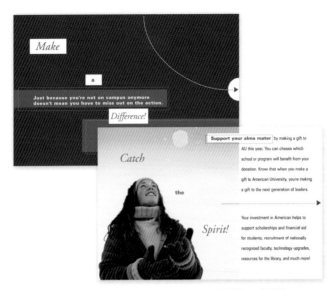

Design Firm: American University, Washington DC **Client:** AU Office of Development **Title:** Catch the Spirit! **Designer:** Maria Jackson

Design Firm: Anita Soos Design, Stony Creek CT **Title:** Hugh O'Donnell B.U. Show Catalog **Art Director:** Anita Soos **Designer:** Anita Soos **Photographers:** Vernon Doucette, Tina Eden, Richard Felber

Design Firm: Avicom Marketing Communications, Waukesha WI **Client:** Harley- Davidson Financial Services **Title:** Epay Dealer Campaign **Art Director:** Laura Bernarde **Designer:** Laura Bernarde

Design Firm: Behan Communications, Glens Falls NY **Client:** Glens Falls Hospital Foundation **Title:** All the Money in the World... **Art Director:** Troy Burns **Designer:** Mik Bondy **Photographers:** Tom Grow, Craig Murphy

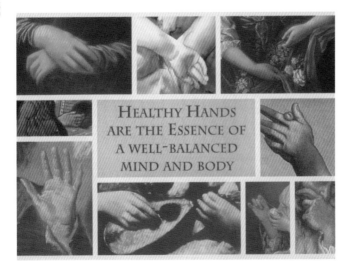

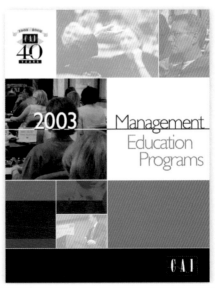

Design Firm: C&C Graphics, Malverne NY **Client:** Queensboro Occupational Therapy **Title:** Promo Mailer **Art Director:** Lisa L. Cangemi **Designer:** Lisa L. Cangemi

Design Firm: CAI Communications, Raleigh NC **Client:** Capital Associated Industries **Title:** Seminar Catalog **Art Director:** Steve McCulloch **Designer:** Debra Rezeli **Photographer:** Pete Hutson

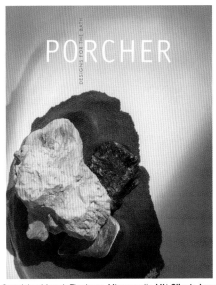

Design Firm: Carmichael Lynch Thorburn, Minneapolis MN **Client:** American Standard
Title: Porcher Catalog **Creative Director:** Bill Thorburn **Designer:** Wit Vongsangiam
Photographers: Earl Kendall, Steve Henke, John Mowers

Design Firm: Carmichael Lynch Thorburn, Minneapolis MN **Client:** Formica
Title: Flooring **Creative Director:** Michael Skjei **Designer:** Travis Olson
Photographer: Scott Dorrance

Design Firm: Charming Shoppes, Bensalem PA **Client:** Fashion Bug **Title:** Bra Mailer
Art Director: Lisbeth Harding **Designer:** Derek Jolly **Photographer:** Carol Weinberg
Copy Chief: Kristen Kearney-Argow

Design Firm: Chelsea Direct Marketing, Putnam Valley NY **Client:** Langenscheidt
Publishers **Title:** Hammond American Map Catalog **Art Director:** Wendy M. Whetsel
Designer: Wendy M. Whetsel **Photographer:** Hank Azzato

Design Firm: Chen Design Associates, San Francisco CA **Client:** Joe Goode
Performance Group **Title:** Folk Direct Mail Season Campaign **Art Director:** Joshua C.
Chen **Designer:** Joshua C. Chen **Photographer:** RJ Muna, CDA Archives

Design Firm: Cisneros Design, Santa Fe NM **Client:** Senor Murphy
Title: Mini Catalog **Art Director:** Brian Hurshman **Designer:** Yvette Jones
Illustrator: Paul Mirocha

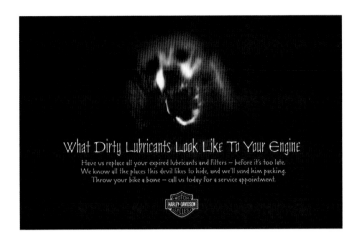

Design Firm: Computer Associates International Inhouse Creative Development, Islandia NY **Client:** Corporate Associates International **Title:** FlexSelect Cardboard Man Direct Mail **Art Director:** Loren Moss Meyer **Designer:** Loren Moss Meyer **Photographers:** Franz and Peter Edson

Design Firm: DCI Marketing, Milwaukee WI **Client:** Harley-Davidson **Title:** RPM Service Reminder **Art Director:** Alan Eliason **Designer:** Alan Eliason **Illustrator:** Alan Eliason **Copywriters:** Alan Eliason, Mark Hembree

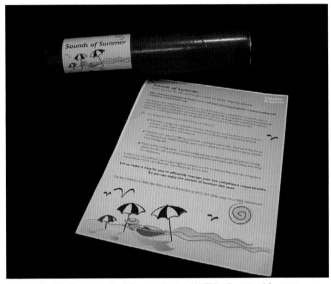

Design Firm: Debra Malinics Advertising, Philadelphia PA **Client:** Chancellor Park **Title:** Chancellor Park **Art Director:** Debra Malinics **Designer:** Debra Malinics **Photographers:** Various

Design Firm: Deloitte & Touche, Boston MA **Title:** Sounds of Summer **Art Director:** Barbara Calautti **Designer:** Natalie Salls

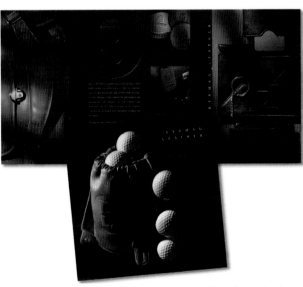

Design Firm: DesignWorks NY, LLC, New York NY **Client:** Pitney Bowes **Title:** Pitney Perks Solicitation **Art Director:** Kelley Briggs **Designers:** Kelley Briggs, Miriam Schroeder

Design Firm: Designwrite Advertising, Excelsior MN **Client:** Berman Leather **Title:** Golf Collection Catalog **Art Director:** Steve Siewert **Designer:** Steve Siewert **Photographer:** Scott Knutson

Design Firm: Division Street Design, Westlake OH **Client:** Hickory Hill
Title: Direct Mail Postcard **Designer:** Cynthia Peterson **Copywriter:** Christine Lobas

Design Firm: Division Street Design, Westlake OH **Client:** Western Enterprises
Title: Medica Catalog **Art Director:** Cynthia Peterson **Designers:** Cynthia Peterson,
Jana Vinadia, Chris Clotz

Design Firm: Emily Rich Design, Encino CA **Client:** Bureau of Jewish
Education L.A. **Title:** Youth Programs Postcard Campaign **Art Director:** Emily Rich
Camras **Designer:** Emily Rich Camras

Design Firm: Federated Marketing Services, New York NY
Client: Federated Merchandising Group **Title:** Alfani Mailers
Art Director: Axel Celikates **Photographer:** Iris Brosch

Design Firm: Gary Taylor Creative Group, Los Angeles CA **Client:** Jafra Cosmetics
International **Title:** Jafra Body Catalog **Art Director:** Gary Taylor
Designer: Elaine Weathers **Photographers:** Paul Rumohr, Jeff Sarpa

Design Firm: Greenhouse Design, Highland Park NJ **Client:** Pharmacia Group
Title: Direct Mail **Art Director:** Miriam Grunhaus **Designer:** Miriam Grunhaus

Design Firm: Hanlon Brown Design, Portland OR **Client:** Adidas **Title:** Original Merchandise Plan **Art Directors:** Sandy Brown, Cindy Brandt **Designer:** Cindy Brandt

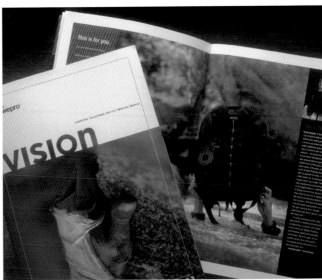

Design Firm: Hornall Anderson Design Works, Seattle WA **Client:** Lowepro **Title:** Catalog **Art Director:** John Anicker **Designers:** Mary Hermes, Dorothee Soechting, Andrew Wicklund, Gretchen Cook **Photographers:** Various

Design Firm: Hornall Anderson Design Works, Seattle WA
Client: Seattle SuperSonics **Title:** Marketing Folder **Art Director:** Jack Anderson
Designers: Jack Anderson, Andrew Wicklund, Mark Popich

Design Firm: ImageSmith Advertising, Bridgewater NJ **Client:** B. Braun Medical
Title: Injekt Direct Mailer **Art Director:** Candice Silva **Designer:** Candice Silva

Design Firm: Interactive Network for Continuing Education (INCE),
Cranbury NJ **Title:** Look Where Innovation Can Take You
Art Director: Jamie Santiago **Designer:** Jamie Santiago

Design Firm: International Paper, Memphis TN **Title:** DEFOR Postcard Family
Art Director: Roger Rasor **Designer:** Shea Morgan

Design Firm: Island Oasis, Walpole MA **Title:** National Mailer **Art Director:** Jennifer Howard **Designer:** Jennifer Howard **Photographer:** Peter Buhler

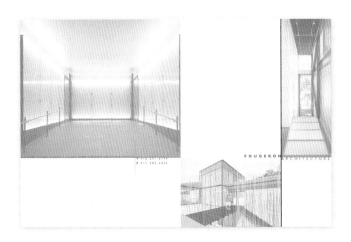

Design Firm: Ison Design, San Francisco CA **Client:** Fougeron Architecture **Title:** Presentation Folder

Design Firm: Kichler Lighting, Cleveland OH **Title:** Kichler House Beautiful Catalog **Art Directors:** Todd Langner, Kim Napier, Michael Byers **Designer:** Michael Byers **Photographers:** Kalman & Pabst Photo Group

Design Firm: Kircher Inc., Washington DC **Client:** International Association of Amusement Parks and Attractions **Title:** IAAPA Orlando Tabloid **Art Director:** Bruce E. Morgan **Designers:** Bruce E. Morgan, John Frantz, Lisa Garrison **Photographer:** Tina Williams

Design Firm: Laughing Stock, South Newfane VT **Title:** Catalog No. 10 **Designer:** Carol Ross **Illustrators:** Gordon Studer (cover) and various (inside)

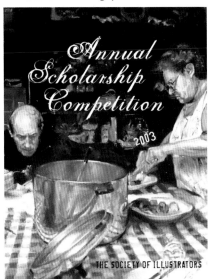

Design Firm: Multipod, Brooklyn NY **Client:** The Society of Illustrators **Title:** Annual Scholarship Competition Catalog **Art Director:** Randi Hazan **Designer:** Randi Hazan **Illustrators:** Various **Photographer:** Client

Design Firm: O'Neal Design, St. Louis MO Client: Micky's Minis Flora Express Title: Catalog Art Director: Steve O'Neal Designers: Steve O'Neal, Tibor Nagy Photographer: Don Casper

Design Firm: Out of the Box Marketing, Hoffman Estates IL Client: United Stationers Title: Direct Mail Art Director: Brad Pencil Designer: Kerri Kuzel

Design Firm: Paragraphs Design, Chicago IL Client: Unisource Title: Topkote Paper Brochure Art Director: Meow Vatanatumrak Designer: Meow Vatanatumrak Photographer: Karen Cipolla

Design Firm: Pearson Learning Group, Parsippany NJ Title: Nonfiction Catalog Art Director: Linda Hoffman Designer: Angel Devost, Devost Design Photographers: Various

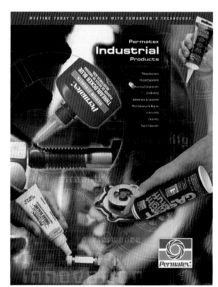

Design Firm: Permatex Inc., Hartford CT Title: Industrial Products Catalog Art Director: Lauren Mencarini Designer: Lauren Mencarini Photographers: Marty Blieker, Ken Davis, Lauren Mencarini, Dick Smolinski, Jeffrey Yardis

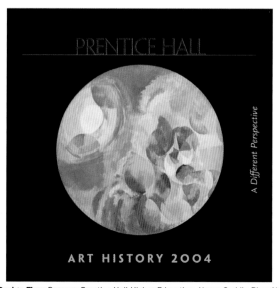

Design Firm: Pearson Prentice Hall Higher Education, Upper Saddle River NJ Client: Prentice Hall Title: Art History: A Different Perspective Art Director: Robert Farrar-Wagner Designer: Robert Farrar-Wagner

Design Firm: PreVision, Lincoln MA **Client:** Stride Rite **Title:** New Moms Mailer
Art Directors: Michael Chrisner, George Lepore **Designers:** Floyd Sipe, Carla Arriaga
Photographer: Ross Whitaker **Writer:** Diana Kirk

Design Firm: Ricoh Corporation, West Caldwell NJ **Title:** Premium Golf Program
Art Director: Wendy Helft **Designer:** C + T Artworks **Photographer:** Tom Kosa

Design Firm: Scana Corporation, Columbia SC **Client:** SCE&G Residential Marketing
& Sales **Title:** There's a Better Way **Art Directors:** Melissa H. Meadows, Alex
Sargeant **Designer:** Melissa H. Meadows **Photographer:** George Fulton

Design Firm: Shrine Design, Chelsea MA **Client:** Workbookstock
Title: Synthesia **Designer:** Adam Larson

Design Firm: Smith & Dress, Huntington NY **Client:** Olympus America
Title: Education Catalog **Designers:** Fred and Abby Dress

Design Firm: Tartan Marketing, Maple Grove MN **Client:** Cargill Health
and Food Technologies **Title:** Direct Mail **Designers:** Linda Thiltgen,
Barry McCullough **Writer:** Amy Rae Mason

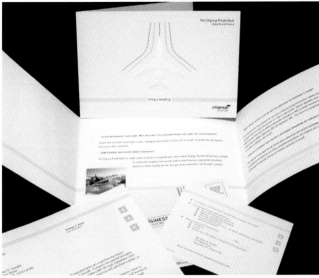

Design Firm: The Citigroup Private Bank, New York NY **Client:** Global Aircraft Finance
Title: Global Aircraft Direct Mail **Designer:** Dado Lam

Design Firm: The College Board, New York NY **Title:** Key Resources for Counselors
Designer: Liz Buckley

DIRECT MAIL AND DIRECT RESPONSE

Design Firm: Tin Yen Studios, Alhambra CA **Client:** UCLA **Title:** UCLA Extension
Open House **Art Director:** Tin Yen **Designer:** Tin Yen

Design Firm: Tribune Media Services, Chicago IL **Client:** KRT Campus **Title:** KRT
Campus Postcard **Designer:** Matt Maldre **Illustrators:** Various **Photographers:** Various

Design Firm: Veer, Calgary AB and Provo UT **Title:** Veer Visual Elements Catalog
Art Director: Sheldon Popiel **Designers:** Bryce Beresh, Sheldon Popiel, Grant
Hutchinson **Copywriter:** Jon Parker

Design Firm: ZGraphics, Ltd., East Dundee IL **Client:** ASAP Software
Title: Microsoft.NET Direct Mail Piece **Art Director:** Joe Zeller
Designer: Kris Martinez Farrell **Illustrator:** Turnbaugh Illustration

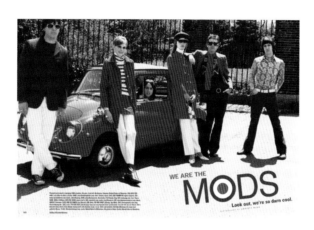

EDITORIAL DESIGN

BOOKS | NEWSLETTERS | PUBLICATIONS

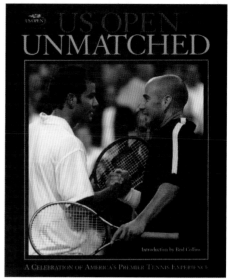

Design Firm: Junie Osaki Design, Pasadena CA **Client:** Manuscript Originals/Andrews McMeel Pub. **Title:** Off the Record **Art Director:** Junie Osaki **Designer:** Junie Osaki **Photographers:** Various

Design Firm: Kirsten Navin Design, Fairfield CT **Client:** United States Tennis Association **Title:** US Open Unmatched **Art Director:** Kirsten Navin

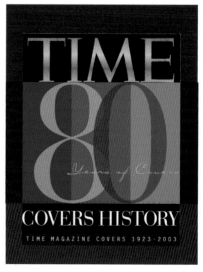

Design Firm: Nuwave Design, Dix Hills NY **Client:** Saint Elizabeth Church **Title:** 40th Jubilee Directory **Art Director:** Christine Armstrong **Designer:** Christine Armstrong

Design Firm: Roni Lagin Graphic Design, Philadelphia PA **Client:** Fanfare Publishing Inc. **Title:** Love You Live, Rolling Stones **Art Director:** Roni Lagin **Designer:** Roni Lagin

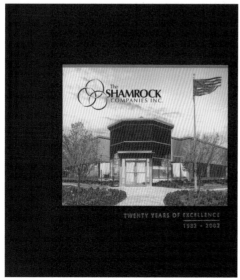

Design Firm: The Shamrock Companies, Westlake OH **Title:** History Book **Art Directors:** Dave Larson, John Bennett **Designer:** Lori Leiter

Design Firm: Time Magazine/Time Marketing, New York NY **Client:** Time Magazine **Title:** Time Covers History **Creative Services Director:** Liza Greene **Art Director:** Andrea Costa **Illustrator:** Andrea Costa

Design Firm: VMA Inc., Dayton OH Client: Montgomery County
Historical Society Title: Dayton Comes of Age Art Director: Kenneth Botts
Designer: Al Hidalgo Photographer: NCR Archives

Design Firm: Volume Design, San Francisco CA Client: CCAC Wattis Institute
for Contemporary Arts Title: Rock My World Exhibit Catalog Designer: Eric Heiman
Photographers: Various

Design Firm: Warner Books, New York NY Title: If Looks Could Kill
Art Director: Jacki Merri Meyer Designer: Shasti O'Leary Soudant

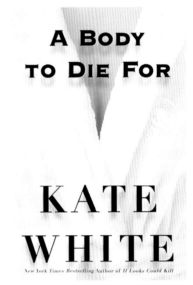

Design Firm: Warner Books, New York NY Title: A Body To Die For
Art Director: Jacki Merri Meyer Designer: Shasti O'Leary Soudant

Design Firm: Addison, New York NY Client: Viacom Title: Upfront
Art Director: David Kohler Designer: John Moon

Design Firm: Artisa LLC, Plainsboro NJ Client: Stuart Country Day School
of the Sacred Heart Title: The Tartonian Newsletter, Vol. No. 2 Art Director: Isabella
D. Palowitch Designer: Isabella D. Palowitch Photographer: Laura Novia

Design Firm: Baltimore Area Convention and Visitors Association (BACVA), Baltimore MD **Title:** BACVA Newsletter **Designer:** Georganne Cammarata

Design Firm: Behan Communications, Glens Falls NY **Client:** Finch Pruyn & Co. **Title:** Finch Paper **Art Director:** Troy Burns **Designer:** Troy Burns **Photographer:** Gary Golde

Design Firm: Creative Fusion Design Company, Branford CT **Client:** GE Business Credit **Title:** Lending Report **Art Director:** Craig Des Roberts **Designer:** Craig Des Roberts

Design Firm: Edward Jones, St. Louis MO **Client:** Edward Jones **Title:** Investment Insight **Art Director:** Brian Hopwood **Designer:** Mark Stagner

Design Firm: Franke + Fiorella, Minneapolis MN **Client:** Thrivent **Title:** Financial Edge **Art Director:** Craig Franke **Designer:** Richard Ketelsen **Illustrators:** Various **Photographers:** Various

Design Firm: Mary T. Altobelli, Chester NY **Client:** Arts Community Grants of Orange County **Title:** Art Space **Art Director:** Mary T. Altobelli **Designer:** Mary T. Altobelli

Design Firm: Morehead Dotts & Associates, Corpus Christi TX
Client: Driscoll Children's Health Plan **Title:** Chip News
Art Director: Roy Smith **Designer:** Gilbert Cantu

Design Firm: Perry A. Graphics, Vernon Hills IL **Client:** Save-a-Pet
Title: Paws for Thought Newsletter **Designer:** Perry Anderson

Design Firm: Star One Credit Union, Sunnyvale CA **Title:** Fall Newsletter
Art Director: Richard A. Bogucki **Designer:** Richard A. Bogucki

Design Firm: The Humane Society of the United States, Gaithersburg MD
Title: Wild Neighbors News **Art Director:** Paula Jaworski **Designer:** Christine Edwards

Design Firm: UP Design LLC, Montclair NJ **Client:** Organon Pharmaceuticals
Title: Dialogue **Art Director:** Carin Manetti **Designer:** Wendy Peters
Photographers: Mike Krinke, Dennis Conners, Phil Leo

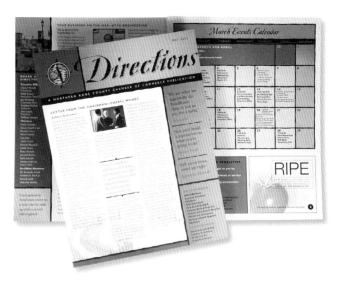

Design Firm: ZGraphics, Ltd., East Dundee IL **Client:** Northern
Kane County Chamber of Commerce **Title:** Directions NewsLetter
Art Director: LouAnn Zeller **Designer:** Nate Baron

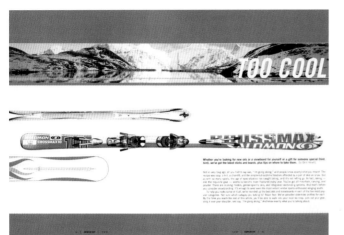

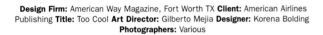

Design Firm: American Way Magazine, Fort Worth TX **Client:** American Airlines Publishing **Title:** Too Cool **Art Director:** Gilberto Mejia **Designer:** Korena Bolding **Photographers:** Various

Design Firm: American Way Magazine, Fort Worth TX **Client:** American Airlines Publishing **Title:** Go Wild **Art Director:** Gilberto Mejia **Designer:** Charles Stone **Photographer:** David Muench

Design Firm: American Way Magazine, Fort Worth TX **Client:** American Airlines Publishing **Title:** George Stephanopoulos' D.C. **Art Director:** Gilberto Mejia **Designer:** Gilberto Mejia **Photographer:** Justin Case

Design Firm: American Way Magazine, Fort Worth TX **Client:** American Airlines Publishing **Title:** Alternative Autos **Art Director:** Gilberto Mejia **Designer:** Korena Bolding

Design Firm: American Way Magazine, Fort Worth TX **Client:** American Airlines Publishing **Title:** Islands Less Traveled **Art Director:** Gilberto Mejia **Designer:** Charles Stone **Photographer:** Neil Selkirk

Design Firm: American Way Magazine, Fort Worth TX **Client:** American Airlines Publishing **Title:** Jamie Lee Curtis' Los Angeles **Art Director:** Gilberto Mejia **Designer:** Charles Stone **Photographer:** Art Streiber

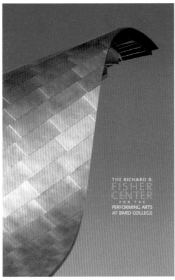

Design Firm: Bard College Publications, Annandale-On-Hudson NY **Client:** The Richard B. Fisher Center For the Performing Arts at Bard College **Title:** Fisher Center Opening Program **Art Director:** Mary Smith **Designer:** Michael Elrod

Design Firm: Business Travel News, New York NY **Client:** In-House VNU **Title:** Business Travel Buyer's Handbook **Art Director:** Teresa M. Carboni **Designer:** Teresa M. Carboni **Illustrator:** Sandy Nichols, 3-In-A-Box

Design Firm: Custom Publishing Group, Cleveland OH **Client:** The Leading Edge Alliance **Title:** The Leading Edge Publication **Art Director:** Amanda Horvath **Designer:** Amanda Horvath **Illustrator:** Brian Willse

Design Firm: Custom Publishing Group, Cleveland OH **Client:** COSE (Council Of Smaller Enterprises) **Title:** Update Magazine **Art Director:** Amanda Horvath **Designer:** Amanda Horvath

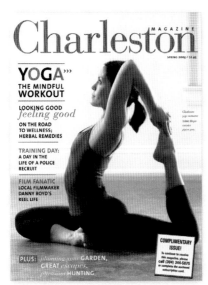

Design Firm: Custom Publishing Group, Cleveland OH **Client:** Charleston WVA Convention & Visitor's Bureau **Title:** Charleston Magazine **Art Director:** Stacy Vickroy **Designer:** Stacy Vickroy **Photographer:** Rick Lee (cover)

Design Firm: Dever Designs, Laurel MD **Client:** Psychotheraphy Networker **Title:** Brain Therapy **Art Director:** Jeffrey L. Dever **Designer:** Jeffrey L. Dever **Illustrator:** Jerzy Kolacz

Design Firm: Dever Designs, Laurel MD Client: Front Porch Magazine
Title: December Art Director: Chris Komisar Designers: Chris Komisar,
Jeffrey L. Dever Illustrator: Robert Tanenbaum

Design Firm: Dever Designs, Laurel MD Client: Liberty Magazine
Title: Sex Lies & Ethics Art Director: Jeffrey L. Dever Designer: Jeffrey L. Dever
Illustrator: Scott Roberts

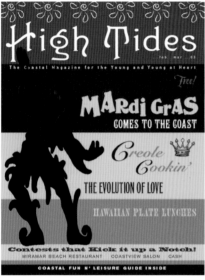

Design Firm: Devious Design, Moss Beach CA Client: High Tides Magazine
Title: Feb/Mar 03 Art Director: Kenneth W. Davis Designer: Kenneth W. Davis
Illustrator: Joanna Bock

Design Firm: Devious Design, Moss Beach CA Client: High Tides Magazine
Title: Apr/May 03 Art Director: Kenneth W. Davis Designer: Kenneth W. Davis
Illustrator: Joanna Bock

Design Firm: Fine Line Design, St. Paul MN Client: Berkeley Lab Title: Highlights
2002-2003 Art Director: Niza Hanany Designer: Niza Hanany Editor: Pam Patterson

Design Firm: Gregory Richard Media Group, Pelham NY Client: Salvation Army
Title: Correction Ministries Art Director: Rich Sohanchyk Designer: Sandra Correa

Design Firm: Hadassah Magazine, New York NY **Title:** January 2003
Art Director: Jodie Rossi **Designer:** Jodie Rossi

Design Firm: K. McGilvery Design, New York NY **Client:** Union Of American Hebrew
Congregations **Title:** Reform Judaism Magazine Spring 2003 **Art Director:** Kathy
McGilvery **Designer:** Kathy McGilvery **Illustrator:** Terry Shoffner (cover)

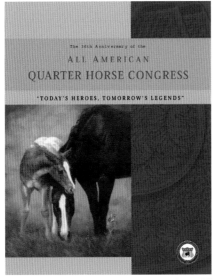

Design Firm: Kelley Communications Group, Dublin OH
Client: Quarter Horse Congress **Title:** Publication Cover
Art Director: Kevin Ronnebaum **Designer:** Betty Czekalski

Design Firm: LifeWay Christian Resources, Nashville TN **Title:** Young Adult &
Collegiate Leader Guide **Art Director:** Angela Brown **Designer:** Angela Brown

Design Firm: Los Alamos National Laboratory, Los Alamos NM
Client: Science and Technology Base Programs **Title:** UCDRD Annual Report Cover
Art Director: Kelly L. Parker **Designer:** Kelly L. Parker

Design Firm: Miller Sports Group Custom Publishing, Fairfield CT
Client: United States Tennis Association **Title:** A Banner Year
Art Director: Kirsten Navin **Designer:** Kirsten Navin

Design Firm: Noon, San Francisco CA **Client:** NAATA **Title:** 21st SFIAAFF Catalog **Art Director:** Cinthia Wen **Designer:** Claudia Fung **Illustrator:** Claudia Fung

Design Firm: Pearson Prentice Hall Higher Education, Upper Saddle River NJ **Client:** Prentice Hall **Title:** Crafting The Very Short Story **Art Director:** Robert Farrar-Wagner **Designer:** Robert Farrar-Wagner **Illustrator:** Steven Kennedy

Design Firm: Popular Mechanics, New York NY **Title:** New Guns of the Old West **Art Director:** Bryan Caniff **Photographer:** Brian Kosoff

Design Firm: Popular Mechanics, New York NY **Title:** New Wheels For The Bravest **Art Director:** Bryan Canniff **Photographer:** Lou Jawitz

Design Firm: Popular Mechanics, New York NY **Title:** Dirty War Cover **Art Director:** Bryan Caniff **Photographer:** James A. Sugar

Design Firm: Popular Mechanics, New York NY **Title:** The Real Face of Jesus **Art Director:** Bryan Caniff

Design Firm: Popular Mechanics, New York NY **Title:** Color My World
Art Director: Bryan Caniff **Photographer:** Greg Alter

Design Firm: Raytheon Technical Services, Burlington MA **Client:** Raytheon
Engineering and Technology **Title:** Technology Today **Art Director:** Susan DeCrosta
Designer: Susan DeCrosta **Photographers:** Dana Aaby, Rick Marickovich

Design Firm: Ricoh Corporation, West Caldwell NJ **Title:** Image Magazine-
Charting the Future **Art Director:** Richard A. Muller **Designer:** Richard A. Muller
Illustrator: Frank Avellino

Design Firm: Rutgers, The State University of New Jersey, New Brunswick NJ
Client: Foundation Relations **Title:** Partnerships **Art Director:** Joanne Dus-Zastrow
Designer: Joanne Dus-Zastrow **Illustrator:** David Pohl

Design Firm: Rutgers, The State University of New Jersey, New Brunswick NJ
Client: Rutgers University Foundation **Title:** Creating the Future Today **Art Director:**
Joanne Dus-Zastrow **Designer:** Joanne Dus-Zastrow **Illustrator:** Valerie Sinclair
Photographer: Nick Romanenko

Design Firm: The Improper Bostonian, Boston MA **Title:** How to be a Blue Man
Art Director: Scott Oldham **Photographer:** James Porto

Design Firm: RMS, Newark CA **Client:** RMS **Title:** Exposure Magazine Cover Series
Art Director: John Abraham **Designer:** Yaping Xie **Illustrator:** Yaping Xie

Design Firm: U.S. General Accounting Office, Washington DC **Client:** GAO
Title: Performance and Accountability Report **Designers:** Barbara Hills, Leo Barbour
Illustrators: Barbara Hills, Leo Barbour **Photographer:** Rocky Rockburn

Design Firm: USA Weekend, McLean VA **Title:** Your Wonderful New Baby
Creative Manager: Casey Shaw **Art Director:** David Baratz
Designer: Leon Lawrence III **Photographers:** Jens Lucking and various

Design Firm: USA Weekend, McLean VA **Title:** Spring Home & Garden Issue
Creative Manager: Casey Shaw **Art Director:** David Baratz **Designer:** Pamela Smith
Photographer: Alan Goldstein

Design Firm: USA Weekend, McLean VA **Title:** Spring Fashion Issue
Creative Manager: Casey Shaw **Art Director:** David Baratz **Designer:** Leon Lawrence III
Photographers: Kevin Masur, Michael Dwornik, Carlos Serrao

Design Firm: Wolken Communica, Seattle WA **Title:** Blurred@Coca
Art Director: Kurt Wolken **Designer:** Kurt Wolken **Photographer:** Lara Swimmer

Design Firm: YM Magazine, New York NY **Client:** YM Magazine/G & J Publishing
Title: Nelly Furtado **Art Director:** Amy Demas **Designer:** Anton Ioukhnovets
Photographer: Joseph Cultice

Design Firm: YM Magazine New York NY **Client:** YM Magazine/G & J Publishing
Title: The Mysterious Mr. Wood **Art Director:** Amy Demas **Designer:** Amy Demas
Photographer: Sheryl Nields

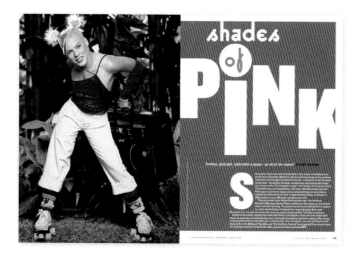

Design Firm: YM Magazine, New York NY **Client:** YM Magazine/G & J Publishing
Title: Shades of Pink **Art Director:** Amy Demas **Designer:** Amy Demas
Photographer: Joseph Cultice

Design Firm: YM Magazine, New York NY **Client:** YM Magazine/G & J Publishing
Title: In the Blazer **Art Director:** Amy Demas **Illustrator:** Istvan Banyai

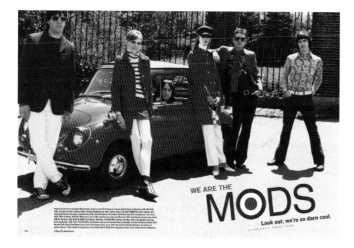

Design Firm: YM Magazine, New York NY **Client:** YM Magazine/G & J Publishing
Title: We Are the Mods **Art Director:** Amy Demas **Designer:** Amy Demas
Photographer: Christy Bush

Design Firm: ZGraphics Ltd., East Dundee IL **Client:** Aurora Area Convention &
Visitor Bureau **Title:** Visitor Guide **Art Director:** Joe Zeller **Designer:** Renee Clark

IDENTITY DESIGN

CORPORATE IDENTITY SYSTEMS I LETTERHEAD AND STATIONERY I LOGOS

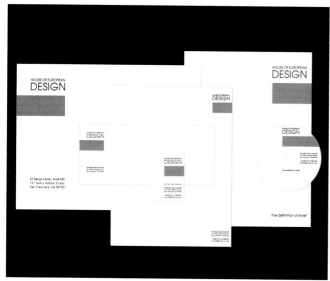

Design Firm: Artenergy, Kentfield CA **Client:** House Of European Design
Title: Corporate Identity **Art Director:** Aliona Sanarina **Designer:** Martin S. Wolf

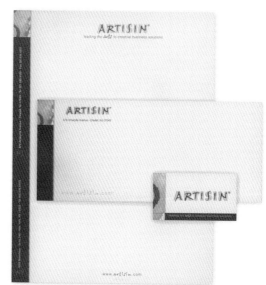

Design Firm: Barnett Design, Inc., Ramsey NJ **Client:** ARTISIN, LLC
Title: Identity Kit **Art Director:** Debra Barnett Sagurton
Designers: Jefferson Ramos, Aparna Mulchandani

Design Firm: Barnett Design, Inc., Ramsey NJ **Client:** Aesthetically Yours
Title: Aesthetically Yours Kit **Art Director:** Debra Barnett Sagurton
Designer: Jefferson Ramos

Design Firm: C. Sogard Visual Think, Salt Lake City UT **Client:** Jones
Waldo Holbrook & McDonough Attorneys & Counselors **Title:** Corporate Identity
Art Director: Carol Sogard **Designer:** Carol Sogard

Design Firm: Cisneros Design, Santa Fe NM **Client:** Dentistry for Kids
Title: Letterset Package **Art Director:** Eric Griego **Designer:** Eric Griego
Illustrator: Eric Griego

Design Firm: Creative AIM, Southport CT **Client:** Pepsi **Title:** Mountain Dew Look
Book **Art Director:** Ann Lumpinski **Designer:** Rich Phillips **Illustrator:** Stan Kay

Design Firm: Debra Malinics Advertising, Philadelphia PA **Client:** Accenture **Title:** New Frontiers Welcome Kit **Art Director:** Debra Malinics **Designer:** Joe Mercatante

Design Firm: Debra Malinics Advertising, Philadelphia PA **Client:** RubinGoldman and Associates **Title:** RubinGoldman ID **Art Director:** Debra Malinics **Designer:** Debra Malinics

Design Firm: Division Street Design, Westlake OH **Client:** Norwalk Furniture **Title:** Norwalk PIT Crew **Art Director:** Jana Vanadia **Designer:** Jana Vanadia

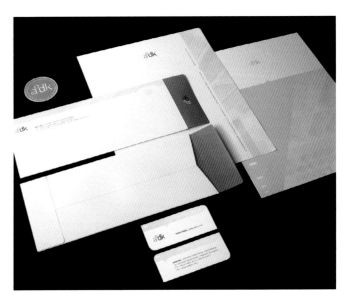

Design Firm: Flourish, Cleveland OH **Client:** AODK: Architecture Office David Krebs **Title:** Identity System **Art Directors:** Christopher Ferranti, Jing Lauengco, Henry Frey **Designer:** Steve Shuman

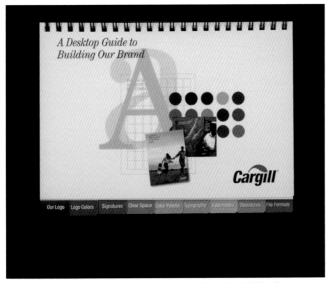

Design Firm: Franke + Fiorella, Minneapolis MN **Client:** Cargill **Title:** Corporate Identity (Desktop) **Art Director:** Craig Franke **Designers:** Leslie McDougall, Richard Ketelsen, Todd Monge **Illustrators:** Leslie McDougall, Richard Ketelsen, Todd Monge **Photographers:** Various

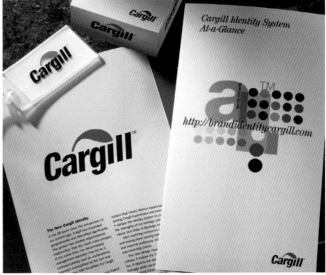

Design Firm: Franke + Fiorella, Minneapolis MN **Client:** Cargill **Title:** Corporate Identity **Art Director:** Craig Franke **Designers:** Leslie McDougall, Richard Ketelsen, Todd Monge **Illustrators:** Leslie McDougall, Richard Ketelsen, Todd Monge **Photographers:** Various

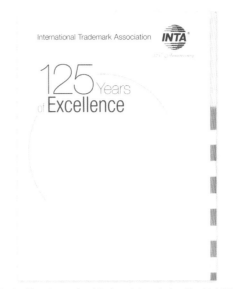

Design Firm: Group One, Minneapolis MN **Client:** Parsinen Kaplan Rosberg & Gotlieb P.A. **Title:** Leave Behind Kit for Law Firm **Art Director:** Jennifer Meelberg **Designer:** Jennifer Meelberg

Design Firm: International Trademark Association, New York NY **Title:** Media Kit **Designer:** David Sokolosky

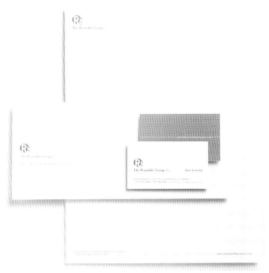

Design Firm: Jones Design Group, Atlanta GA **Client:** The Reynolds Group **Title:** Identity **Art Director:** Vicky Jones **Designer:** Katherine Staggs

Design Firm: Michael Osborne Design, San Francisco CA **Client:** Gymboree **Title:** Janie & Jack Series **Art Director:** Michael Osborne **Designer:** Michael Regenbogen

Design Firm: Nautica International, New York NY **Title:** Coporate Idenity Program **Art Director:** Ray Murray **Designers:** Carol Kushniruk, Kevin Sparrok

Design Firm: OrangeSeed Design, Minneapolis MN **Client:** Lori Nesvoid Massage Therapy **Title:** Stationery Program **Art Director:** Damien Wolf **Designer:** Damien Wolf

Design Firm: Page Design Inc., Sacramento CA **Client:** J.P. Heintz & Co., Inc.
Title: Corporate ID **Art Director:** Paul Page **Designer:** Tracy Titus
Illustrators: Jen Rafanan, Brian Johnson

Design Firm: Patricia Vogt Graphic Design, Chicago IL **Client:** Yes Print Management
Title: Presentation Package **Art Director:** Patricia Vogt **Designer:** Patricia Vogt

Design Firm: Pepsi-Cola Design Group, Purchase NY **Title:** Pepsi Look Book
Art Director: Marion Schneider **Designers:** Marion Schneider and Creative Aim

Design Firm: Plymouth Printing Co., Cranford NJ **Title:** Corporate Identity
Art Director: Coleen M. Catrino **Designer:** Coleen M. Catrino

Design Firm: RG Creations Inc., San Carlos CA **Client:** eBay **Title:** Brand Guidelines
Designer: Cardinal O'Neill **Illustrator:** Stephen Schudlich

Design Firm: Sayles Graphic Design, Des Moines IA **Title:** Big Brothers
Big Sisters of Central Iowa **Art Director:** John Sayles **Designer:** Som
Inthalangsy **Illustrator:** John Sayles

Design Firm: Splinter Group, Sayreville NJ **Client:** Maxim Group **Title:** Identity System
Art Director: Rob Adams **Designer:** Rob Adams **Photographer:** John Decker

Design Firm: The Bancorp Bank, Wilmington DE **Title:** Corporate Presentation Folder
Art Director: Amy Holt **Designer:** Amy Holt

Design Firm: Accentuate Inc., Santa Fe Springs CA **Title:** Stationery System
Art Director: Laurie Schiada **Designers:** Danny Tong, Bret Chambers, Gloria Hall

Design Firm: Arketype Inc., Green Bay WI **Client:** Little Tokyo **Title:** Letterhead &
Stationery **Art Director:** Jim Rivett **Designer:** DeGaull Vang

Design Firm: BBK Studio, Grand Rapids MI **Client:** Holland Area Arts Council
Title: Identity System **Art Director:** Kevin Budelmann **Designer:** Alison Popp

Design Firm: Brand New Minds, Ft. Lauderdale FL **Title:** Stationery
Art Directors: Raelene Mercer, Andrew Smith **Designer:** Raelene Mercer

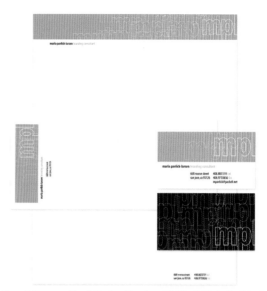

Design Firm: CAI Communications, Raleigh NC **Client:** Triangle Industry
Liaison Group **Title:** TILG Letterhead 13 **Art Director:** Steve McCulloch
Designer: Debra Rezeli

Design Firm: Cathereene Huynh Design, San Jose CA **Client:** Maria Pavlick, Branding
Consultant **Title:** MPL Business Stationery System
Art Director: Cathe Huynh-Sison **Designer:** Cathe Huynh-Sison

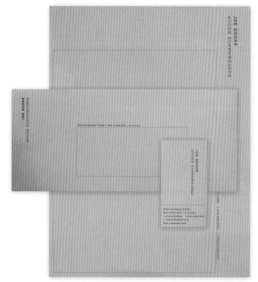

Design Firm: Chen Design Associates, San Francisco CA **Client:** Joe Goode
Performance Group **Title:** Letterhead & Biz Cards **Art Director:** Joshua C. Chen
Designer: Kathryn Hoffman

Design Firm: Christina Balas, Long Branch NJ **Client:** Tomaino Tomaino
Iamello & Associates **Title:** TTIa Stationery **Designer:** Christina Balas

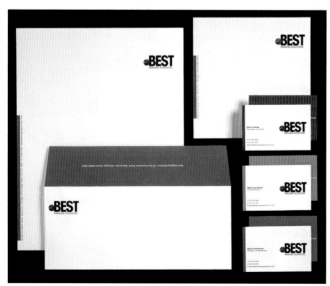

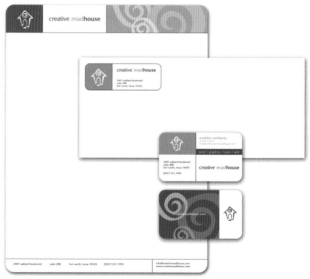

Design Firm: Cochran + Associates, Chicago IL **Client:** Best Imaging Solutions
Title: Letterhead & Stationery **Art Director:** Bobbye Cochran **Designer:** Bobbye
Cochran **Illustrator:** Bobbye Cochran

Design Firm: Creative Madhouse, Forth Worth TX **Title:** Stationery Package
Art Director: Madelyn Wattigney **Designer:** Madelyn Wattigney
Illustrator: Madelyn Wattigney

Design Firm: Division Street Design, Westlake OH **Client:** PricePoint Partners
Title: Stationery **Art Director:** Chris Clotz **Designer:** Chris Clotz

Design Firm: Douglas Hill, Northborough MA **Client:** GIG/Graphic Idea Group
Title: Letterhead & Stationery **Designers:** Doug Hill, Gene Zukowski, Lesley Breen
Winthrow **Illustrator:** Lesley Breen Winthrow

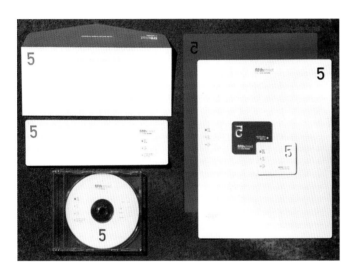

Design Firm: Fifth Street Design, Minneapolis MN **Title:** Identity
Designers: Dan West, Erin Mason, Dan Voorhees

Design Firm: Flourish, Cleveland OH **Client:** AODK: Architecture Office David Krebs
Title: Letterhead **Art Directors:** Christopher Ferranti, Jing Lauengco, Henry Frey
Designer: Steve Shuman **Photographer:** Steve Shuman

Design Firm: Galperin Design Inc., New York NY **Client:** Temenos Villas
Title: Stationery **Art Director:** Peter Galperin **Designer:** Kristina Paukulis

Design Firm: Gunnar Swanson Design Office, Ventura CA **Client:** Midtown
Ventura Community Council **Title:** Stationery **Art Director:** Gunnar Swanson
Designer: Gunnar Swanson

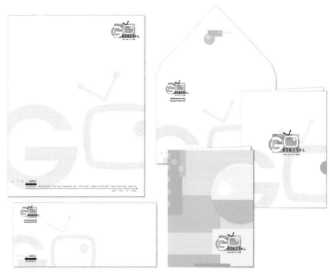

Design Firm: Gunnar Swanson Design Office, Ventura CA **Title:** Stationery
Art Director: Gunnar Swanson **Designer:** Gunnar Swanson

Design Firm: Kelley Communications Group, Dublin OH **Client:** WOSU
Title: Go Digital Letterhead **Art Director:** Kevin Ronnebaum **Designer:** Betty Czekalski

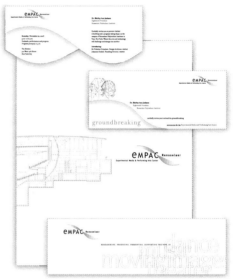

Design Firm: KRE8IVE Design, Cleveland OH **Client:** Hahn & Pollock,
Counselors at Law **Title:** Stationery System **Art Director:** Joseph S. Kovach
Designer: Joseph S. Kovach

Design Firm: Odgis + Co., New York NY **Client:** EMPAC Rensselaer
Title: Identity System **Art Director:** Janet Odgis **Designers:** Janet Odgis,
Wilfredo Cruz, Banu Berker

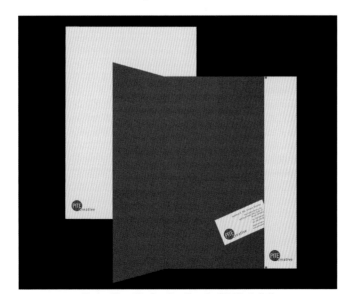

Design Firm: Pite Creative, Superior CO **Client:** Self
Title: Letterhead **Designer:** Jonathan Pite

Design Firm: Steffian Bradley Architects, Boston MA **Title:** Letterhead and Stationery
Art Director: Rob Silsby **Designer:** Rob Silsby

Design Firm: t.a. design, Burlington NJ **Client:** Sports & Specialist Cars **Title:** Sports & Specialist Cars Stationery **Art Director:** T.A. Hahn **Designer:** T.A. Hahn

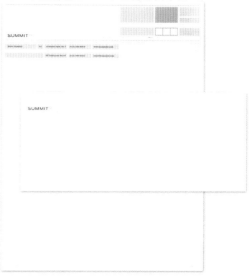

Design Firm: Templin Brink Design, San Francisco CA **Client:** Summit Identity Design **Title:** Stationery System **Art Directors:** Joel Templin, Gaby Brink **Designer:** Brian Gunderson

Design Firm: Tribune Media Services, Chicago IL **Client:** VUE **Title:** VUE Letterhead **Art Director:** Jill Sherman

Design Firm: Veer, Calgary AB and Provo UT **Title:** Letterhead and Stationery **Art Director:** Sheldon Popiel **Designers:** Bryce Beresh, Sheldon Popiel

Design Firm: Accentuate Inc., Santa Fe Springs CA **Title:** Grafico Inc. Logo **Art Director:** Laurie Schiada **Designers:** Laurie Schiada, Brent Reid

Design Firm: Accentuate Inc., Santa Fe Springs CA **Client:** Audio Visual Services Corp. **Title:** AVSC Identity System **Art Director:** Laurie Schiada **Designer:** Steve Gross

Design Firm: Acme Communications, New York NY Client: Michael Rubin Architects
Title: Logo Design Designer: Kiki Boucher Illustrator: Kiki Boucher

Design Firm: Acronym Design, Peoria IL Title: Logo
Designer: Nadine Cole Illustrator: Nadine Cole

EGYPTIAN COTTON

Design Firm: Andrea Costa, New York NY Client: DAI-USAID for Egypt
Title: Egyptian Cotton Logo/J. Silberman Art Director: Andrea Costa
Illustrator: Andrea Costa

LITTLE TOKYO
JAPANESE CUISINE & SUSHI BAR

Design Firm: Arketype Inc., Green Bay WI Client: Little Tokyo Title: Logo
Art Director: Jim Rivett Designer: DeGaull Vang

Arizant
Healthcare
bright ideas that work

Design Firm: Arizant Healthcare Inhouse Design, Minneapolis MN Client: Arizant
Healthcare Title: Healthcare Logo Art Director: Mike Miller Designer: Mike Miller

Bair Paws™

Patient Adjustable Warming System

Design Firm: Arizant Healthcare Inhouse Design, Minneapolis MN Client: Arizant
Healthcare Title: Bair Paws Logo Art Director: Mike Miller Designer: Mike Miller

Design Firm: atCommunications LLC, Oakbrook Terrace IL
Client: OurFootDoctor.com Title: Logo Designer: Terry P. Kasdan

Design Firm: Avicom Marketing Communications, Waukesha WI Client: MDA
Title: Black-n-Blue Ball 2003 Art Director: Jeff McCulloch Designer: Jeff McCulloch

Design Firm: BBK Studio, Grand Rapids MI Client: SitOnIt Seating Title: SitOnIt
Identity Art Director: Yang Kim Designers: Yang Kim, Michele Chartier, Alison Popp,
Kevin Budelmann, Sharon Oleniczak Illustrator: Yang Kim

Design Firm: Be.Design, San Rafael CA Client: The Stinking Rose
Restaurant Title: The Stinking Rose Identity Art Director: Eric Read
Designers: Lisa Brussel, Coralie Russo

Design Firm: Be.Design, San Rafael CA Client: Creekside Title: Photo TLC Identity
Art Director: Eric Read Designers: James Eli, Yuseke Asaka Illustrator: Corinne Brimm

Design Firm: Be.Design, San Rafael CA Client: Artsopolis Title: San Jose Art Council
Identity Art Director: Will Burke Designers: Yusuke Asaka, Monica Schlaug

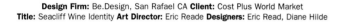

Design Firm: Be.Design, San Rafael CA **Client:** Cost Plus World Market
Title: Seacliff Wine Identity **Art Director:** Eric Reade **Designers:** Eric Read, Diane Hilde

Design Firm: Be.Design, San Rafael CA **Client:** Frontier Natural Products
Title: Simply Organic Identity **Art Director:** Will Burke **Designers:** Eric Read,
Suzanne Hadden, Monica Vallejos **Illustrator:** Will Nelson

Design Firm: Be.Design, San Rafael CA **Client:** Mighty Leaf Tea
Company **Title:** Mighty Leaf Identity **Art Directors:** Will Burke, Eric Read
Designers: Coralie Russo, James Elii

Design Firm: Behan Communications, Glens Falls NY **Client:** Cost Control Associates
Title: Logo **Art Director:** Troy Burns **Designer:** Jane Gould

Design Firm: Bill Zillmer, Madison WI **Client:** Bella Hair Salon
Title: Hair Salon Logo **Designer:** Bill Zillmer

Design Firm: Bracchi Design, New York NY **Client:** JW Pet Company Inc.
Title: activitoys Logo **Art Director:** Theresa Bracchi **Designer:** Theresa Bracchi

Your source for hard-to-find computer equipment

Design Firm: Brook-Schwartz Design Studio, San Diego CA **Client:** CodeMicro
Title: Logo **Art Director:** Denise Brook-Schwartz **Illustrator:** Denise Brook-Schwartz

Design Firm: BTW Design, Huntington Beach CA **Client:** Huntington Culinary Inc.
Title: Bringing Home...Home Logo **Art Director:** Becky Tee Ward **Designer:** Becky Tee
Ward **Illustrator:** Becky Tee Ward

Design Firm: BTW Design, Huntington Beach CA **Client:** SunnLaine
Artisans **Title:** Logo **Art Director:** Becky Tee Ward **Designer:** Becky Tee Ward
Illustrator: Becky Tee Ward

Design Firm: CAI Communications, Raleigh NC **Client:** North Carolina Dental Society
Title: Conference Logo **Art Director:** Beth Greene **Designer:** Beth Greene

Design Firm: CAI Communications, Raleigh NC **Client:** Unique Tile and Stone
Title: Logo **Art Director:** Steve McCulloch **Designer:** Debra Rezeli

Design Firm: Cairril.Com Design, Bloomington IN **Client:** Parke Williams Ltd.
Title: Logo **Designer:** Cairril Mills

Design Firm: Carmichael Lynch Thorburn, Minneapolis MN Client: AT Cross
Title: ION Creative Director: Michael Skjei Designer: David Schrimpf

Design Firm: Carmichael Lynch Thorburn, Minneapolis MN Client: AT Cross
Title: Verve Creative Director: Michael Skjei Designer: David Schrimpf

Design Firm: Christina Balas, Long Branch NJ Client: Tomaino Tomaino
Iamello & Associates Title: Squiggle Logo Designer: Christina Balas

Design Firm: Cisneros Design, Santa Fe NM Client: Bumble Bee's Baja Grill Title: Logo
Art Director: Brian Hurshman Designer: Yvette Jones Illustrator: Beth Berriman

Design Firm: Cisneros Design, Santa Fe NM Client: Anasazi Restaurant Title: Logo
Art Director: Fred Cisneros Designer: Fred Cisneros Calligrapher: Jane Dill

Design Firm: Cisneros Design, Santa Fe NM Client: Jackalope Title: Logo
Designer: Fred Cisneros Illustrator: Joel Nakamura

CMP
United Business Media

Design Firm: CMP Media LLC, Manhasset NY Client: CMP Title: Logo
Art Director: Brian A. McClean Designer: Brian A. McClean

hāzel

Design Firm: Cochran + Associates, Chicago IL Client: Hazel (Boutique) Title: Logo
Art Director: Bobbye Cochran Designer: Bobbye Cochran Illustrator: Bobbye Cochran

Design Firm: Computer Associates International Inhouse Creative Development,
Islandia NY Title: Compass Club Logo Designer: Malia Vrooman
Illustrator: Malia Vrooman

Design Firm: Creative Fusion Design Company, Branford CT Client: IDG World Expo
Title: BioIT World Logo Art Director: Craig Des Roberts Designer: Craig Des Roberts

Design Firm: Creative Fusion Design Company, Branford CT Client: License Monitor Inc.
Title: Company Logo Art Director: Chris Walsh Designer: Chris Walsh

Design Firm: Creative Instinct, Denver CO Client: San Angelo Saints Professional
Hockey Organization Title: Logo Art Director: Gavin Levy Designer: Shawn Watson
Illustrator: Shawn Watson

Design Firm: Cuff Creative, Mount Laurel NJ **Client:** Philadelphia Tax Conference **Title:** PTC Tax Logo **Art Director:** Michelle Cuff **Designer:** Robert Cuff **Illustrator:** Robert Cuff

Design Firm: DeForest Creative, Elmhurst IL **Client:** ITL WRK, Ltd. **Title:** Montage Restaurant Logo **Art Director:** Wendy Weaver **Designer:** Wendy Weaver **Photographer:** Kim Hurdlebrink

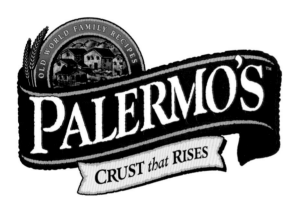

Design Firm: Design North, Racine WI **Client:** Palermo's **Title:** Palermo's Pizza **Art Director:** Pat Cowan **Designer:** Pat Cowan **Illustrator:** Art Grebetz

Design Firm: Deutsch Design Works, San Francisco CA **Client:** Anheuser-Busch **Title:** Crown B Budweiser Logo **Creative Director:** Barry Deutsch **Art Director:** John Marota, AB Image Development **Designers:** Greg Perin, Eric Pino

Design Firm: Devi-Designs, Indianapolis IN **Client:** BroadWave Technologies Inc **Title:** Logo **Art Directors:** Devi Haripal, Mike Trulock **Designer:** Devi Haripal **Illustrator:** Devi Haripal **Photographer:** Devi Haripal

Design Firm: Division Street Design, Westlake OH **Client:** Broadcast Media Ideas **Title:** Logo **Art Director:** Chris Clotz **Designer:** Chris Clotz **Illustrator:** Chris Clotz

EdwardJonesDome

Design Firm: Edward Jones, St. Louis MO **Client:** Edward Jones **Title:** Facilities ID for Edward Jones Dome **Art Director:** Bart Crosby **Designer:** Crosby Associates

Design Firm: Elements, Hamden CT **Client:** Arts Council of Greater New Haven **Title:** ArtSpot **Art Director:** Amy Wentworth **Designer:** Amy Wentworth

Design Firm: Emily Rich Design, Encino CA **Client:** University of Judaism **Title:** Sigi Ziering Institute for the Study of the Religious & Moral Implications of the Holocaust **Art Director:** Emily Rich Camras **Designer:** Emily Rich Camras **Illustrator:** Emily Rich Camras

Design Firm: Evenson Design Group, Culver City CA **Client:** Binney and Smith/Crayola **Title:** Big Yellow Box Trademark **Art Director:** Stan Evenson **Designers:** Kera Scott, Glenn Sakamoto

Design Firm: Faith Design, Mamaroneck NY **Client:** Willow Capital Management **Title:** Logo **Art Director:** Faith E. Deegan **Designer:** Faith E. Deegan

Design Firm: Fitzgerald Esplin Advertising, New Hope PA **Client:** Pharmaceutical Resource Corporation **Title:** Logo **Designer:** Ingela Nader

Design Firm: Fitzgerald Esplin Advertising, New Hope PA **Client:** Apex Communications **Title:** Logo **Art Director:** Joanne Esplin **Designer:** Lisa McGettigan

Design Firm: Flourish, Cleveland OH **Client:** AODK: Architecture Office David Krebs **Title:** Logo **Art Directors:** Christopher Ferranti, Jing Lauengco, Henry Frey **Designers:** Steve Shuman, Lisa Ferranti **Photographer:** Steve Shuman

DKW COMMUNICATIONS, INC.

Capitol Hill
BUSINESS & TAX SERVICES, INC.

Design Firm: Flowers Creative Group Graphic Communications, Cheverly MD **Client:** DKW Communications, Inc. **Title:** Logo **Art Director:** Shawn Yvette Flowers **Designer:** Shawn Yvette Flowers

Design Firm: Flowers Creative Group Graphic Communications, Cheverly MD **Client:** Capital Hill Business & Tax Services, Inc. **Title:** Logo **Art Director:** Shawn Yvette Flowers **Designer:** Shawn Yvette Flowers

Design Firm: Flowers Creative Group Graphic Communications, Cheverly MD **Client:** Humphrey International, Inc. **Title:** Logo **Art Director:** Shawn Yvette Flowers **Designer:** Shawn Yvette Flowers

Design Firm: Flowers Creative Group Graphic Communications, Cheverly MD **Client:** Skyclub @ Zanzibar On The Waterfront **Title:** Logo **Art Director:** Shawn Yvette Flowers **Designer:** Shawn Yvette Flowers

BROKAW

Rising by the River

Design Firm: Foth & Van Dyke, Green Bay WI **Client:** Village Of Brokaw
Title: Logo **Designer:** Daniel Green **Illustrator:** Daniel Green

Design Firm: Franke + Fiorella, Minneapolis MN **Client:** Cargill **Title:** Logo
Art Director: Craig Franke **Designer:** Craig Franke **Illustrator:** Leslie McDougall

Amistad

Design Firm: Gabriela Gasparini Design, Brooklyn NY **Client:** Amistad-An Imprint
of Harper Collins Publishers **Title:** Logo **Art Director:** Gabriela Gasparini
Designer: Gabriela Gasparini **Illustrator:** Gabriela Gasparini

Design Firm: Generator Studios, West Chester PA
Client: October Frost Enterprises **Title:** Logo **Art Director:** Scott Beard
Designer: Rich Hunsinger **Illustrator:** Rich Hunsinger

Design Firm: Ginkgo Creative, Chicago IL **Client:** Diversity Initiatives
Title: Logo **Art Director:** Gina Luoma **Designers:** Gina Luoma, Katie Rundell
Illustrator: Ginkgo Creative

Design Firm: Greenhouse Design, Highland Park NJ **Client:** Exhale Massage Therapy
Title: Logo Design **Art Director:** Miriam Grunhaus **Designer:** Miriam Grunhaus

Design Firm: Gregory Richard Media Group, Pelham NY **Client:** Sublink **Title:** Logo **Art Director:** Rich Sohanchyk **Designer:** Ron Mohan

Design Firm: Gregory Richard Media Group, Pelham NY **Client:** Integrated Technology Associates, Inc. **Title:** Logo **Art Director:** Rich Sohanchyk **Designer:** Ron Mohan

Design Firm: Group One, Minneapolis MN **Client:** American Express Financial Services **Title:** WMS Mark **Art Director:** Zion Wu Anderson **Designer:** Dan Nichols

Design Firm: Group T Design, Washington DC **Client:** The Wood Rack **Title:** Logo **Art Director:** Tom Klinedinst **Designer:** Tom Klinedinst **Illustrator:** Tom Klinedinst

Design Firm: Group T Design, Washington DC **Client:** Blue Water Media **Title:** Logo **Art Director:** Tom Klinedinst **Designer:** Tom Klinedinst **Illustrator:** Tom Klinedinst

Design Firm: Gunnar Swanson Design Office, Ventura CA **Client:** Midtown Ventura Community Council **Title:** Logo **Art Director:** Gunnar Swanson **Designer:** Gunnar Swanson

JASNA
Los Angeles 2004

Design Firm: Gunnar Swanson Design Office, Ventura CA
Client: Jane Austen Society Of North America **Title:** Logo
Art Director: Gunnar Swanson **Designer:** Gunnar Swanson

BioTrek

Design Firm: Gunnar Swanson Design Office, Ventura CA
Client: California State Polytechnic University, Pomona **Title:** BioTrek Logo
Art Director: Gunnar Swanson **Designer:** Gunnar Swanson

2004

Biathlon World Cup

FORT KENT, MAINE U.S.A.

Design Firm: Heidesign, Fort Kent ME **Client:** Maine Winter
Sports Center **Title:** World Cup Logo **Art Director:** Heidi Carter
Designer: Heidi Carter **Illustrator:** Heidi Carter

HIDA2003
MEDSURG
CONFERENCE & EXPO™
The Medical Products Marketplace

OCTOBER 2–4, 2003 • BALTIMORE, MARYLAND
BALTIMORE CONVENTION CENTER

Design Firm: HIDA (Health Industry Distributors Association),
Alexandria VA **Title:** 2003 MedSurg Logo **Designer:** Wendy Brewer

Design Firm: Hornall Anderson Design Works, Seattle WA
Client: Pace International **Title:** Pace Idenity **Art Director:** Jack Anderson
Designers: Jack Anderson, Sonja Max, Andrew Smith

Design Firm: Hornall Anderson Design Works, Seattle WA **Client:** ActiveWear
Title: Identity **Art Director:** Jack Anderson **Designers:** Kathy Saito, Gretchen Cook

R A V E N   C O A S T

great wines ⊷ unique gifts

Design Firm: Howard Designs, Kirkland WA Client: Raven Coast
Producers Title: Logo Designer: Jason Howard Illustrator: Jason Howard

Design Firm: Innovative Advertising, LLC, Covington LA Client: Juice Fine
Wines Title: Juice Logo Art Director: Elizabeth Guidry Badeaux
Creative Director: Jay Connaughton Designer: Elizabeth Guidry Badeaux
Illustrator: Elizabeth Guidry Badeaux

TRANSPORTATION™
COMMUNICATIONS, LLC

Design Firm: Inova Health System, Springfield VA Client: Inova
Health System Foundation Title: Gala Signature Art Director: Nancy Johnston
Designer: Catalyst Design

Design Firm: Intelligent Fish Studio, Palatine IL Client: Transportation
Communications, LLC Title: Logo Art Director: Brian Danaher
Designer: Brian Danaher, Brian Pirman

Design Firm: International Paper, Memphis TN Client: Sun Valley
Pecan Company Title: Sun Valley Pecan Company Logo Art Director: Roger Rasor
Designer: Terry Jarred Illustrator: Terry Jarred

Design Firm: Keck Garrett Associates, Chicago IL Client: Orange Glo International
Title: Oxi Clean Logo Redesign Art Director: Cher Garrett Designer: Shelbi Gabriel

Design Firm: Kelley Communications Group, Dublin OH **Client:** WOSU
Title: GO Digital Logo **Art Director:** Kevin Ronnebaum **Designer:** Betty Czekalski

Design Firm: Kennedy & Associates, Cincinnati OH **Client:** Global Food
Industries **Title:** Logo **Art Director:** Matt Fearn **Designers:** Deb Laber, Matt Fearn
Photographer: Teri Studios

Design Firm: KO11 Inc., East Brunswick NJ **Client:** Point Pleasant ShockWave
Title: Logo **Art Director:** John Ko **Designer:** John Ko **Illustrator:** Man Yee Cheng

Design Firm: Laura Coe Design Associates, San Diego CA **Client:** CJS Lighting
Title: Logo **Art Director:** Laura Coe Wright **Designer:** Tracy Castle

Design Firm: Lentini Design, Los Angeles CA **Client:** Crusade for Animals
Title: Logo **Art Director:** Hilary Lentini **Designer:** Hilary Lentini

Design Firm: Lorenc+Yoo Design, Roswell GA **Client:** Woodstock Baptist Church
Title: Baptist Church Logo Design **Art Director:** Jan Lorenc **Designer:** Chung Yoo

Design Firm: Los Alamos National Laboratory, Los Alamos NM **Client:** Health, Safety, and Radiation Protection Division **Title:** Logo **Designer:** Stacey Castro

Design Firm: Michael Osborne Design, San Francisco CA **Client:** U.S. Postal Service **Title:** Love Stamp **Art Director:** Ethel Kessler **Designer:** Michael Osborne

Design Firm: Miller Sports Group Custom Publishing, Fairfield CT **Client:** Tennis Magazine **Title:** Demo Days **Art Director:** Kirsten Navin **Illustrator:** Kirsten Navin

Design Firm: Mimi Braatz & Associates, San Jose CA **Client:** South Valley Developers **Title:** Quail Creek Logo **Art Director:** Jill McCoy **Designer:** Jill McCoy **Illustrator:** Jill McCoy

Design Firm: Minx Design, Akron OH **Client:** 7 West Inc. **Title:** Logo **Designer:** Cecilia M. Sveda

Design Firm: Minx Design, Akron OH **Client:** Four Points Architectural Services, Inc. **Title:** Logo **Designer:** Cecilia M. Sveda

Design Firm: Money's Worth Advertising, Cranford NJ **Client:** Parq Business Development **Title:** Parq Logo **Designers:** Dennis Miller, Joe Tozzolino

Design Firm: NHL Creative Services, New York NY **Client:** NHL Events & Entertainment **Title:** League Meetings Logo **Art Directors:** Paul Conway, Kathy Drew **Designer:** Paul Conway

Design Firm: NHL Creative Services, New York NY **Client:** NHL Fan Development **Title:** Street Fit Program **Art Directors:** Paul Conway, Kathy Drew **Designer:** Paul Conway

Design Firm: Oakley Design Studios, Portland OR **Client:** Physical Element **Title:** Symbol **Art Director:** Tim Oakley **Designer:** Tim Oakley **Illustrator:** Tim Oakley

Design Firm: Out of the Box Marketing, Hoffman Estates IL **Client:** Big C **Title:** Logo **Designer:** Brad Pencil

Design Firm: PaperMouse, Maple Grove MN **Client:** Amplio Marketing **Title:** Integrity Health Care Logo **Designer:** Shelly Hokel

Design Firm: Pepsi-Cola Design Group, Purchase NY **Title:** Pepsi Logo
Art Director: Marion Schneider **Designers:** Marion Schneider, Sherry Voytek,
John Mierisch **Illustrator:** Ice Pond Studio

Design Firm: Perreault Design, Brooklyn NY **Client:** I Openers **Title:** Logo
Art Director: Michelle Perreault **Designer:** Michelle Perreault

Design Firm: Philippe Becker Design, San Francisco CA **Client:** Whole Foods Market
Title: 365 Organic Logo **Art Director:** Philippe Becker **Designer:** Philippe Becker

Design Firm: Proverb Associates, Palos Heights IL **Client:** Steelhead Corp.
Title: Logo **Designer:** Michael Piper

Design Firm: Proverb Associates, Palos Heights IL **Client:** Women in Graphic
Media & Technology **Title:** Logo **Designer:** Christine Gravel

Design Firm: Q Collective, East Elmhurst NY **Client:** Athletic Business Conference
Title: Logo **Art Director:** Sandie Maxa **Designer:** Mark Sanders

LOGOS, TRADEMARKS AND SYMBOLS

RIGHTSYDE GRAPHICS INC.
MEDIACOMMUNICATION

Design Firm: Rightsyde Graphics Inc., Fayetteville GA **Title:** Logo
Art Director: Mark A. Mackey **Designer:** Mark A. Mackey **Illustrator:** Mark A. Mackey

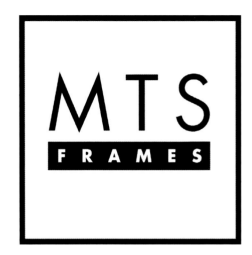

Design Firm: Ronald Ridgeway, Montclair NJ **Client:** MTS Frames Inc.
Title: MTS Frames Logo **Art Director:** Ronald Ridgeway **Designer:** Priya Harracksingh

DESTINY DANCE
international

Design Firm: Rule29, Elgin IL **Client:** Destiny Dance International
Title: Logo **Art Director:** Justin Ahrens **Designers:** Justin Ahrens,
Elecia Gilstrap **Illustrator:** Elecia Gilstrap

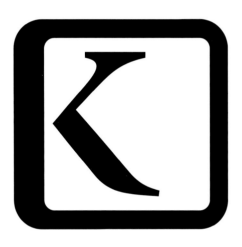

Design Firm: Saturn Flyer, Alexandria VA **Client:** Kryptosima
Title: Logo **Designer:** Jim Gay

TURTLE BAY
TOWERS

Design Firm: Sherman Advertising, New York NY **Client:** Rockrose **Title:** Turtle Bay
Towers Logo **Art Director:** Sharon Lloyd McLaughlin **Designer:** William Touchet

ONE
SEAPORT
PLAZA
199 WATER STREET

Design Firm: Sherman Advertising, New York NY **Client:** Jack
Resnick & Sons **Title:** One Seaport Plaza Logo **Art Director:** Sharon Lloyd
McLaughlin **Designer:** William Touchet

A Professional Corporation

Design Firm: The Bailey Group, Plymouth Meeting PA **Client:** The Jewish Home & Hospital **Title:** Identity **Art Directors:** Steve Perry, Dave Fiedler **Designers:** Christian Williamson, Wendy Slavish

Design Firm: The Bailey Group, Plymouth Meeting PA **Client:** Old Orchard **Title:** Identity **Art Directors:** Steve Perry, Dave Fiedler **Designer:** Steve Perry

UNIVERSITYSQUARE

Design Firm: The Bailey Group, Plymouth Meeting PA **Client:** University of Pennsylvannia **Title:** Identity **Art Directors:** Steve Perry, Dave Fiedler **Designer:** Jerry Corcoran

Design Firm: The Bailey Group, Plymouth Meeting PA **Client:** Life & Health of America **Title:** Identity **Art Director:** Dave Fiedler **Designers:** Jerry Corcoran, Dave Fiedler

Design Firm: Todd M. LeMieux, Springfield MA **Client:** Ludlow Fish Market **Title:** Logo **Art Director:** Todd M. LeMieux **Designer:** Todd M. LeMieux

Design Firm: Towers Perrin, Dallas TX **Client:** Beverly **Title:** PeopleFirst Logo **Art Director:** Eric Redmond **Designer:** Keri Batten **Illustrator:** Keri Batten

Design Firm: Tribune Media Services, Chicago IL **Client:** NewsCom
Title: News Com Logo **Art Director:** Oralia Anderson

Design Firm: Veer, Calgary AB and Provo UT **Title:** Identity/Logo
Art Director: Sheldon Popiel **Designer:** Sheldon Popiel

Design Firm: W Design, New York NY **Client:** African Prison Ministries
Title: Logo **Designer:** Dorene Warner

INTERACTIVE DESIGN AND MOTION GRAPHICS

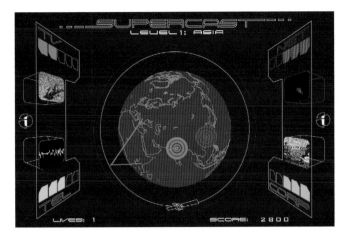

Design Firm: Addison, New York NY Client: Intelsat Title: Supercast Videogame
Art Director: David Kohler

Design Firm: Arketype Inc., Green Bay WI Client: Presto Products Company
Title: Slash 'N Wrap Art Directors: Jim Rivett, Paul Meinke Illustrator: Robb
Mommaerts Animators: Jason Davis, DeGuall Vang

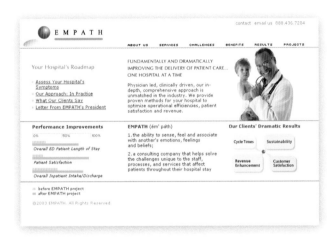

Design Firm: Artenergy, Kentfield CA Client: EMPATH Title: Corporate Website
Art Director: Aliona Sanarina Designer: Sergey Martinov

Design Firm: BMA Media Group, Cleveland OH Client: Winner International Inc.
Title: Juice Batteries Mini CD Art Director: Bob Craig Designer: Bob Craig

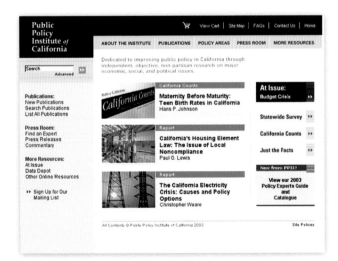

Design Firm: Chen Design Associates, San Francisco CA Client: Public Policy
Institute of California Title: Website Redesign Art Director: Joshua C. Chen
Designers: Brian Singer, Joshua C. Chen

Design Firm: Creative Dynamics Inc., Las Vegas NV Client: Electronic Arts
Title: Command & Conquer Generals Website Art Directors: Casey Corcoran,
Scott Langdon Designers: Casey Corcoran, Scott Langdon Developer: Casey
Corcoran Producer: Scott Langdon

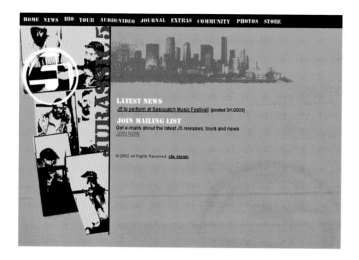

Design Firm: David Salmassian, Orange CA **Client:** Universal Music Group/
The Firm **Title:** Jurassic 5 Website **Art Director:** David Salmassian
Designer: David Salmassian

Design Firm: Del City, Milwaukee WI **Title:** Website **Designer:** Christine Hess

Design Firm: Del City, Milwaukee, WI **Title:** Email Newsletter
Designer: Christine Hess

Design Firm: Design North, Racine WI **Client:** Search Dog **Title:** Website_
Art Director: Gwen Granzow **Designers:** Jane Marcussen, Dave Code

Design Firm: Design360 Inc./Something Digital Llc., New York NY
Client: Grand Central Partnership **Title:** Website Design
Art Director: Enrique Von Rohr **Designer:** Rachel Einsidler

Design Firm: Division Street Design, Westlake OH **Client:** Kellex Corporation
Title: Website **Art Director:** Justin Paluch **Designer:** Justin Paluch

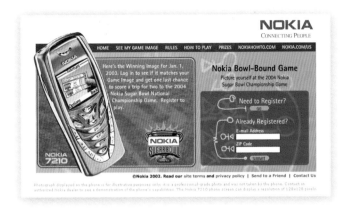

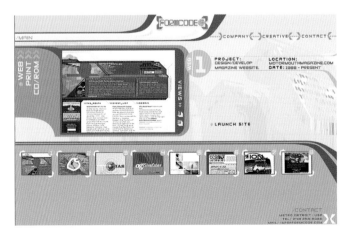

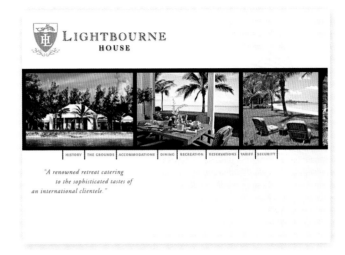

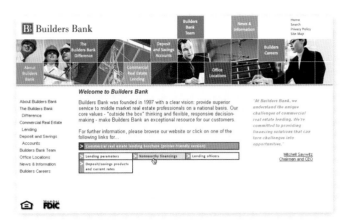

Design Firm: Galperin Design Inc., New York NY **Client:** Lightbourne House
Title: Website **Art Director:** Peter Galperin **Designer:** Peter Galperin
Photographer: Andrew Spreitzer

Design Firm: Galperin Design Inc., New York NY **Client:** Builders Bank
Title: Website **Art Director:** Peter Galperin **Designer:** Peter Galperin

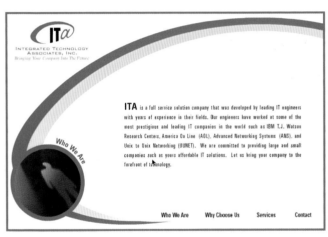

Design Firm: Greenfield Belser Ltd., Washington DC **Client:** Posternak
Blankstein & Feld **Title:** Website **Art Director:** Burkey Belser **Designer:** Lisa Corbett
Illustrator: Tom Cameron **Photographer:** Jason Hendricks

Design Firm: Gregory Richard Media Group, Pelham NY **Client:** Integrated
Technology Associates **Title:** Website **Art Director:** Rich Sohanchyk
Designer: Darren d'Agostino

Design Firm: Hydra Ventures, New York NY **Client:** Hydra Design Build
Title: Corporate Website **Designer:** Maya Amir

Design Firm: Infusion Zone Inc., San Francisco CA **Client:** Casa in iBiza **Title:** Website
Art Director: Chamsi Filali **Designer:** Chamsi Filali **Photographer:** Chamsi Filali

Design Firm: Infusion Zone Inc., San Francisco CA **Client:** SF Friends of the V Foundation **Title:** Jimmy V SF Website **Art Director:** Chamsi Filali **Designer:** Chamsi Filali

Design Firm: International Paper, Memphis TN **Title:** IPDEFOR.com Flash Animation **Art Director:** Roger Rasor **Designer:** Terry Jarred **Illustrator:** Terry Jarred

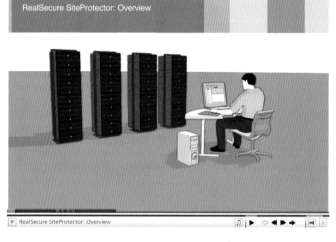

Design Firm: International Paper, Memphis TN **Title:** IPDEFOR.com Website **Art Director:** Roger Rasor **Designer:** Terry Jarred

Design Firm: Mira Design Studio, Atlanta GA **Client:** Internet Security Systems **Title:** RealSecure SiteProtector Demo **Art Directors:** Jackie Dane, Keith Boyd **Designers:** Jackie Dane, Keith Boyd **Illustrator:** Keith Boyd

Design Firm: Morehead Dotts & Associates, Corpus Christi TX **Client:** Dr. Dale Eubank **Title:** Website **Designer:** Roy Smith

Design Firm: Morehead Dotts & Associates, Corpus Christi TX **Client:** Executive Surf Club **Title:** Website **Designer:** Roy Smith **Web Designer:** Janet Wilems

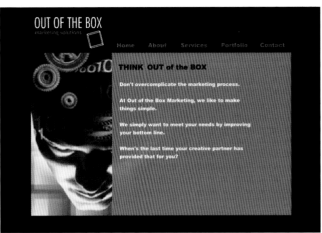

Design Firm: Open Eye Design, Fullerton CA **Client:** Whittier Area Community Church
Title: Website **Art Director:** Greg Herrington **Designer:** Greg Herrington
Photographer: Angelea Toews

Design Firm: Out of the Box Marketing, Hoffman Estates IL **Title:** Website
Art Director: Brad Pencil **Designer:** Kerri Kuzel

Design Firm: Ricoh Corporation, West Caldwell NJ **Client:** Production
Systems Marketing of Ricoh **Title:** Multimedia Overview of Aficio 1060/1075
Art Director: Elisa E. Esposito **Designer:** Elisa E. Esposito

Design Firm: Saturn Flyer, Alexandria VA **Client:** Innov8ive Minds
Title: Website **Designer:** Jim Gay

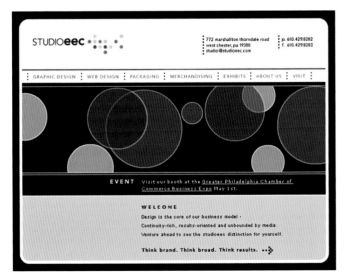

Design Firm: Studioeec, West Chester PA **Client:** Studioeec **Title:** Studioeec Website
Art Directors: Kate Hunsinger, Jorge Del Fabbro **Designers:** Kate Hunsinger, Ken Cox

Design Firm: Tribune Media Services, Chicago IL **Client:** News & Features/TMS
Title: Lola Banner Ads **Designer:** Matt Maldre **Illustrators:** Steve Dickenson, Todd Clark

PACKAGING

Design Firm: Barnett Design, Inc., Ramsey NJ **Client:** Gemini Industries
Title: Gemini Accessories Packaging **Art Director:** Debra Barnett Sagurton
Designer: Jefferson Ramos

Design Firm: Barnett Design, Inc., Ramsey NJ **Client:** Gemini Industries
Title: Hands Free Accessories Packaging **Art Director:** Debra Barnett Sagurton
Designer: Jefferson Ramos

Design Firm: Be.Design, San Rafael CA **Client:** Palm, Inc. **Title:** Palm Packaging
Art Director: Will Burke **Designers:** Coralie Russo, Shinichi Eguchi
Photographer: Richard Seagraves

Design Firm: Be.Design, San Rafael CA **Client:** William-Sonoma Inc.
Title: Easter Packaging **Art Director:** Eric Read **Designers:** Eric Read, Coralie Russo,
Yusuke Asaka **Photographer:** Richard Seagraves

Design Firm: Be.Design, San Rafael CA **Client:** Cost Plus World Market
Title: Seacliff Wine Packaging **Art Director:** Will Burke **Designers:** Eric Read,
Diane Hilde **Illustrator:** Diane Hilde **Photographer:** Richard Seagraves

Design Firm: Be.Design, San Rafael CA **Client:** Mighty Leaf Tea Company
Title: Hotel Amenities **Art Directors:** Will Burke, Eric Read **Designers:** Coralie Russo,
Yusuke Asaka **Photographer:** Yusuke Asaka

Design Firm: Be.Design, San Rafael CA Client: Worldwise, Inc.
Title: Worldwise Packaging System Art Director: Will Burke
Designers: Eric Reed, Shinichi Eguchi Photographer: Wally Bascomb

Design Firm: BMA Media Group, Cleveland OH Client: Winner International Inc. Title:
Juice Battery Packaging Art Directors: Heather Saul, Ray Farrar
Designer: Heather Saul

Design Firm: Brandesign, Monroe NJ Client: Turkey Hill Dairy
Title: Creamy Commotions Art Director: Barbara Harrington Designer: Kevin Tully
Illustrators: Various Photographer: Peter Pioppo (Studio P)

Design Firm: Brandesign, Monroe NJ Client: Bayer Consumer
Healthcare Title: Phillip's Redesign Art Director: Barbara Harrington
Designer: Barbara Harrington

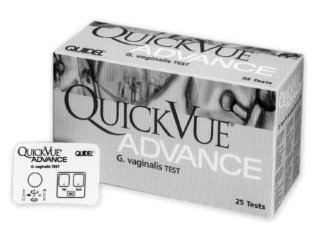

Design Firm: Brandscope, Chicago IL Client: Radio Flyer Title: Specialty Line Carton
Art Director: William Harper Designer: Tim Quirk Illustrator: Steve Lorenz

Design Firm: Brook-Schwartz Design Studio, San Diego CA Client: Quidel Corporation
Title: QuickVue Advance/Woman's Diagnostic For Physician Use
Art Director: Denise Brook-Schwartz Illustrator: Denise Brook-Schwartz

Design Firm: Bryan Williams & Associates, New York NY **Client:** ZenSoy
Title: ZenSoy Pudding **Art Director:** Jeffrey Nucey **Designer:** Mikako Hirata

Design Firm: Carmichael Lynch Thorburn, Minneapolis MN **Client:** Potlatch
Title: Popcorn Box **Creative Director:** Bill Thorburn **Designer:** David Schrimpf

Design Firm: CCBC, Baltimore MD **Title:** Etellicard **Art Director:** Lisa M. Hetrick
Designer: Lisa M. Hetrick **Photographer:** Clark Vandergrift

Design Firm: Charisse McAloon Design, Mt. Prospect IL
Client: Private Perfumery/Designed Exclusively for Target **Title:** FUSION
Designer: Charisse McAloon **Photographer:** Chris Cassidy Photography

Design Firm: Cochran + Associates, Chicago IL **Client:** Isabella Fine Lingerie
Title: Shopping Bags **Art Director:** Bobbye Cochran **Designer:** Bobbye Cochran

Design Firm: Cornerstone Design Associates, New York NY **Client:** Swedish Match
Title: Timberwolf Snuff Packaging Redesign **Art Directors:** Keith Steimel,
Sally Clarke **Designers:** Julia Smith, Sally Clarke **Illustrator:** David O'Neil

Design Firm: Cornerstone Design Associates, New York NY **Client:** Johanna Foods
Title: Ssips Packaging **Art Director:** Sally Clarke **Illustrator:** David O'Neil

Design Firm: Cornerstone Design Associates, New York NY **Client:** Johanna Foods
Title: Tree Ripe Packaging Redesign **Art Director:** Sally Clarke **Designer:** Martin Yeo
Illustrator: David O'Neil

Design Firm: Cornerstone Design Associates, New York NY **Client:** Ambev
Title: Guaraná Soft Drink Packaging Redesign **Art Director:** Sally Clarke
Designer: Martin Teo

Design Firm: Cornerstone Design Associates, New York NY **Client:** Coca-Cola
Title: Sprite Remix Idenity **Art Directors:** Keith Steimel, Sally Clarke
Designer: Martin Yeo **Illustrator:** David O'Neil

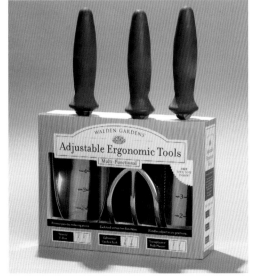

Design Firm: Cull Design Group, Grand Rapids MI **Client:** Whitehall Products
Title: Ergo Tools Package **Art Director:** Scott Millen **Designer:** Allisa Hutchinson
Illustrator: Allisa Hutchinson

Design Firm: Design North, Racine WI **Client:** Scott's **Title:** Scott's Quick Melt
Art Director: Pat Cowan **Designer:** Pat Cowan **Illustrator:** Jeff Mueeler
Photographer: Peter Hernandez

Design Firm: Design North, Racine WI **Client:** Con Agra Foods **Title:** Egg Beaters
Art Director: Gwen Granzow **Designer:** Gwen Granzow **Photographer:** Peter Hernandez

Design Firm: Design North, Racine WI **Client:** Birds Eye Foods **Title:** Voila!
Art Director: Gwen Granzow **Designer:** Jane Marcussen **Photographer:** Peter

Design Firm: Design North, Racine WI **Client:** PTS Labs **Title:** ReVital Packaging
Art Director: Gwen Granzow **Designer:** Dave Code **Illustrator:** Mike Wepplo

Design Firm: Deutsch Design Works, San Francisco CA **Client:** Robert Mondavi
Winery **Title:** Talomas Wine **Art Director:** Barry Deutsch **Designers:** Jess Gambroni,
Lori Wynn **Illustrator:** Lorraine Tuson

Design Firm: Deutsch Design Works, San Francisco CA **Client:** Infinite Spirits
Title: Shakers Vodka **Art Director:** Barry Deutsch **Designers:** Jess Gambroni,
Mike Kunisaki, Lori Wynn

Design Firm: Deutsch Design Works, San Francisco CA **Client:** Pepsi-Cola **Title:** Diet
Pepsi **Art Director:** Barry Deutsch **Designer:** Eric Pino, Pepsi-Cola Design Group

Design Firm: Deutsch Design Works, San Francisco CA Client: Anheuser-Busch
Title: Michelob Ultra Creative Director: Barry Deutsch Art Director: John Marota,
AB Image Development Designer: Eric Pino

Design Firm: Deutsch Design Works, San Francisco CA Client: Pepsi-Cola
Title: Mug Root Beer Art Director: Ron Udiskey Designers: Culver Advertising &
Design/Deutsch Design Works

Design Firm: Di Donato Associates, Chicago IL Client: Terra Harvest
Foods Title: Mr. Krispers Gourmet Rice Chips Art Director: Peter Di Donato
Designers: Peter Di Donato, Doug Miller Illustrator: Doug Miller

Design Firm: Di Donato Associates, Chicago IL Client: Jim Beam Brands
Title: Black Label and Gift Tin Art Director: Peter Di Donato
Designers: Peter Di Donato, Doug Miller Illustrator: Doug Miller

Design Firm: Doug Chatham, Hiram GA Client: Jan Smith Title: Surrender Package
Designer: Doug Chatham Photographers: Beth Parker, Shari Besheers

Design Firm: Duotone Design, Chicago IL Client: Crescent Cardboard LLC
Title: Crescent Digital Paper Packaging Art Director: Katy Moy Designer: Katy Moy

Design Firm: DuPuis, Westlake Village CA **Client:** Foster Farms **Title:** Coastal Range Organics **Art Director:** John Silva **Designer:** John Silva

Design Firm: DuPuis, Westlake Village CA **Client:** Keebler **Title:** Zesta **Art Director:** Steven Dupuis **Designer:** Bill Peirce

Design Firm: DuPuis, Westlake Village CA **Client:** Kellogg's **Title:** Pop-Tarts **Art Director:** Steven Dupuis **Designer:** Bill Peirce

Design Firm: DuPuis, Westlake Village CA **Client:** Bayer **Title:** Ascensia **Art Director:** Bill Corridori **Designer:** Jack Halpern **Illustrator:** Al Nana

Design Firm: DuPuis, Westlake Village CA **Client:** Parmalat's Archway **Title:** Bed & Breakfast **Art Director:** Bill Bless **Designer:** Paul VanDenBerg

Design Firm: DuPuis, Westlake Village CA **Client:** JelSert **Title:** Wyler's Light **Art Director:** Bill Bless **Designer:** Al Nana **Illustrator:** Al Nana

Design Firm: DuPuis, Westlake Village CA **Client:** Kellogg's **Title:** Nutri-Grain Minis
Art Director: Steven DuPuis **Designers:** Al Nana, Jack Halpern

Design Firm: DuPuis, Westlake Village CA **Client:** Keebler **Title:** Chips Deluxe
Art Director: Steven DuPuis **Designer:** Damon Thompson

Design Firm: Earthbound Interactive, Laguna Hills CA **Title:** Interactive CD-ROM
Art Director: Blaine Behringer **Designer:** Brent Kreischer **Illustrator:** Lawrence
Willaford **Photographer:** Jesse Brossa

Design Firm: Eastman Kodak Corporate Design & Usability, Rochester NY
Client: Kodak Professional **Title:** DCS Pro 14N Digital Camera
Art Director: Michelle DeMeyer **Designers:** Michelle DeMeyer, Tim McCann
Photographer: Alan Farkas, Kodak

Design Firm: Eastman Kodak Corporate Design & Usability, Rochester NY **Client:**
Kodak Professional **Title:** Ektatherm 8500 Paper & Ribbon **Art Director:** Michelle
DeMeyer **Designers:** Michelle DeMeyer, Tim McCann **Photographer:** Steve Kelly, Kodak

Design Firm: Evenson Design Group, Culver City CA **Client:** Rocamojo
Title: Packaging **Art Director:** Stan Evenson **Designer:** Kera Scott

Design Firm: FutureBrand, New York NY Client: McNeil Title: Children's Tylenol
Art Director: Stephanie Simpson Designer: Laura Fang Photographer: Ross Whitaker

Design Firm: FutureBrand, New York NY Client: Nestlé Foods
Title: Stouffer's Maxaroni Art Director: Joe Violante Designer: Peter Chieffo
Illustrators: Picture Plane, Mike Wepplo

Design Firm: FutureBrand, New York NY Client: Coca Cola/Nestlé Title: Nestlé
Choglit Chocolate Drink Art Director: Joe Violante Designer: Peter Chieffo

Design Firm: FutureBrand, New York NY Client: Snapple Beverage Group
Title: Snapple Kiwi Teawi Art Director: Joe Violante Designers: Peter Chieffo,
Scott Fisher Illustrators: Mike Wepplo, Tim Shannon

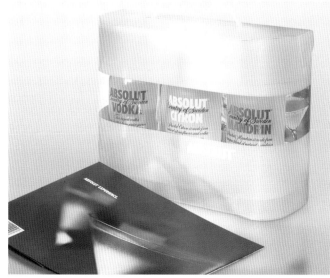

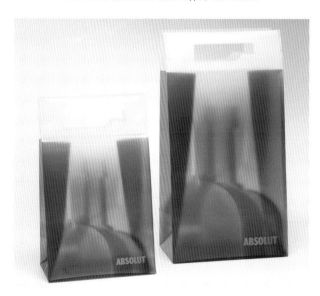

Design Firm: G2 Worldwide, New York NY Client: The Absolut Spirits Company
Title: Absolut 375ml Giftbox Art Director: Andrew Kibble Designer: Maria Samodra
Photographer: Martin Wonnacott

Design Firm: G2 Worldwide, New York NY Client: The Absolut Spirits Company
Title: Absolut Giftbag Art Director: Andrew Kibble Designer: Maria Samodra
Photographer: Martin Wonnacott

Design Firm: H. Montgomery Strategic Design, South Norwalk CT
Client: Snapple Beverage Group **Title:** Elements Aluminum **Art Director:** Hugh
Montgomery **Designer:** Jenna Goguen **Illustrator:** HMS Design

Design Firm: H. Montgomery Strategic Design, South Norwalk CT **Client:** Honeywell
Title: Prestone Appearance Products **Art Director:** Hugh Montgomery
Designer: Josh Laird **Illustrator:** John Watson

Design Firm: H. Montgomery Strategic Design, South Norwalk CT **Client:** Bolthouse
Farms **Title:** Bolthouse Farms 100% Juices **Art Director:** Hugh Montgomery
Designer: Josh Laird **Illustrator:** Heidi Schmidt **Photographer:** Jeff Weir

Design Firm: Hornall Anderson Design Works, Seattle WA **Client:** PMI **Title:** Stanley
Vacuum Sealed Bottles Packaging **Art Director:** Jack Anderson **Designers:** Jack
Anderson, Andrew Wicklund, Henry Yiu, Andrew Smith, Bruce Branson-Meyer

Design Firm: International Paper, Memphis TN **Client:** Costco Wholesale
Title: Premium Grapes DEFOR Family **Art Director:** Roger Rasor **Designer:** Shea
Morgan **Illustrator:** Shea Morgan

Design Firm: International Paper, Memphis TN **Client:** Sun Valley Pecan Company
Title: Pecan Packaging **Art Director:** Roger Rasor **Designer:** Terry Jarred
Illustrator: Terry Jarred

Design Firm: Ionic Communications Group, Cincinnati OH **Client:** Azure Waves Seafood **Title:** Blue Harbor Inn Premium Seafood

Design Firm: Ionic Communications Group, Cincinnati OH **Client:** Changing Paradigms **Title:** Roto Rooter Retail Drain Care

Design Firm: Ionic Communications Group, Cincinnati OH **Client:** Parmalat **Title:** Salerno Cookies

Design Firm: IQ Design Group, New York NY **Client:** Lightlife **Title:** Smart Menu **Art Director:** Leslie Tucker **Designer:** Leslie Tucker **Photographer:** Judd Pilosoff

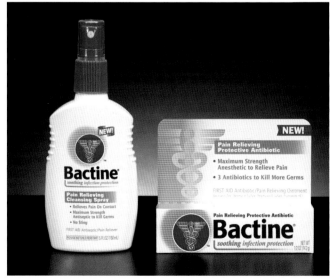

Design Firm: IQ Design Group, New York NY **Client:** Bayer Corporation **Title:** Bactine **Art Director:** Leslie Tucker **Designer:** Darcy Bolker **Illustrator:** Bob Avino

Design Firm: Jodi Eckes-Ads & Art, Anoka MN **Client:** Johnston Inc. **Title:** Honey Soap Packaging **Art Director:** Jodi Eckes **Designer:** Jodi Eckes **Illustrator:** Jeremy Van Tassel

Design Firm: Launch Creative Marketing, Hillside IL Client: Keebler Company
Title: Kellogg's Rice Krispies Treats Halloween Cut Case Wrap Art Director: Michelle
Morales Designer: Bob Howarth Illustrator: Harry Moore

Design Firm: Launch Creative Marketing, Hillside IL Client: Hedstrom Corporation
Title: Mega Sticks Poster Sticker Relaunch Art Director: Brian Spain

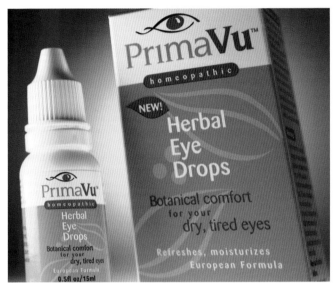

Design Firm: Laura Coe Design Associates, San Diego CA
Client: Bee International/Nestlé Title: Holiday Gift Paks Art Director: Laura Coe
Wright Designer: Tracy Castle Illustrator: Ryoichi Yotsumoto

Design Firm: Laura Coe Design Associates, San Diego CA Client: Prima Pharm Title:
PrimaVu Packaging Art Director: Laura Coe Wright Designer: Tracy Castle

Design Firm: Luis R. Lee & Associates, Suffield CT Client: Friendly Ice Cream
Corporation Title: Holiday and Americana Packaging Art Directors: Heather Van Loan,
Olivia Lee Designer: Luis R. Lee Illustrator: Mark Gerber Photographer: Alan Epstein

Design Firm: Macey Noyes Associates, Wilton CT Client: Acme United
Title: X-Rays Scissors Packaging Art Director: Macey Noyes Associates
Designer: Macey Noyes Associates Illustrator: Macey Noyes Associates
Photographer: Macey Noyes Associates

Design Firm: Macey Noyes Associates, Wilton CT **Client:** Acme United **Title:** X-Rays Scissors Product **Art Director:** Macey Noyes Associates **Designer:** Macey Noyes Associates **Illustrator:** Macey Noyes Associates **Photographer:** Macey Noyes Associates

Design Firm: Macey Noyes Associates, Wilton CT **Client:** Acme United **Title:** Scissor Critters Packaging **Art Director:** Macey Noyes Associates **Designer:** Macey Noyes Associates **Illustrator:** Macey Noyes Associates **Photographer:** Macey Noyes Associates

Design Firm: Macey Noyes Associates, Wilton CT **Client:** Acme United **Title:** Scissor Critters Designs **Art Director:** Macey Noyes Associates **Designer:** Macey Noyes Associates **Illustrator:** Macey Noyes Associates **Photographer:** Macey Noyes Associates

Design Firm: Marsh, Inc., Cincinnati OH **Client:** PLMarketing **Title:** Break-Free **Art Director:** Robert E. Schack **Designer:** Heidi Gray

Design Firm: Marsh, Inc., Cincinnati OH **Client:** Reckitt Benckiser **Title:** Spray 'n Wash **Art Director:** Robert E. Schack **Designer:** Heidi Gray

Design Firm: Melanie Paykos Design, Los Angeles CA **Client:** VH1 **Title:** Liner Notes Packaging **Art Director:** Melanie Paykos **Designer:** Greg Chin

Design Firm: Michael Osborne Design, San Francisco CA **Client:** Alive Enterprises
Title: Old Whiskey River **Art Director:** Michael Osborne **Designer:** Paul Kagiwada

Design Firm: Michael Osborne Design, San Francisco CA **Client:** Brown-Forman
Beverages **Title:** Hard Cola **Art Director:** Michael Osborne **Designer:** Paul Kagiwada

Design Firm: MLR Design, Chicago IL and Pepsi Design Group, Purchase NY
Client: Pepsi-Cola Company **Title:** Wild Cherry Pepsi **Art Director:** Amy Leppet-
Shannon **Designer:** Aaron Funke **Illustrator:** Aaron Funke

Design Firm: MLR Design, Chicago IL and Pepsi Design Group, Purchase NY
Client: Pepsi-Cola Company **Title:** Pepsi Blue **Art Director:** Tom Jones
Designer: Tom Jones **Illustrators:** Tom Jones, Tom Lien

Design Firm: MLR Design, Chicago IL **Client:** Kimberly-Clark**Title:** Huggies Supreme
Art Director: Linda Voll **Designer:** Julie Wineski **Photographer:** Bill Tucker

Design Firm: MLR Design, Chicago IL **Client:** Kaytee Products **Title:** Satori
Art Director: Linda Voll **Designer:** Linda Voll **Illustrator:** Mo Ulicny

Design Firm: MLR Design, Chicago IL **Client:** Hormel Foods **Title:** Hormel Pepperoni
Art Director: Amy Leppert-Shannon **Designer:** Amy Leppert-Shannon
Illustrator: Mike Kasan

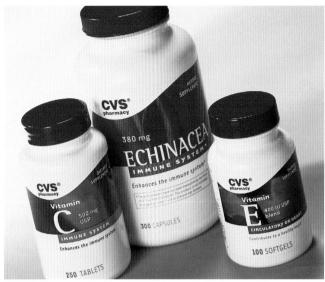

Design Firm: MLR Design, Chicago IL **Client:** CVS Coporation **Title:** CVS OTC
Redesign **Art Director:** Amy Leppert-Shannon **Designer:** Amy Leppert-Shannon

Design Firm: Novo Design Corporation, Red Bank NJ **Client:** Lakeville Cellars,
Oakville CA **Title:** Long Branch Wine Label **Art Director:** Ralph D. Finaldi
Designer: Ty Lindemans

Design Firm: Page Design Inc., Sacramento CA **Client:** Neeruam Inc./Sound & Scent
Title: Packaging **Art Director:** Paul Page **Designers:** Tracy Titus, Irina Staley
Photographer: Robin Walton

Design Firm: Page Design Inc., Sacramento CA **Client:** Club Fresh/Sacramento Salsa
Title: Packaging **Art Director:** Paul Page **Designers:** Tracy Titus, Irina Staley
Illustrator: Irina Staley

Design Firm: Page Design Inc., Sacramento CA **Client:** Chocoholics **Title:** Packaging
Art Director: Paul Page **Designer:** Kimberly Bickel **Illustrator:** Kurt Kland

Design Firm: Page Design Inc., Sacramento CA **Client:** Chocoholics **Title:** Mood Chocolates/Packaging **Art Director:** Paul Page **Designer:** Heather Orr

Design Firm: Pepsi-Cola Design Group, Purchase NY **Title:** Pepsi Redesign **Art Director:** Marion Schneider **Designers:** Marion Schneider, Sherry Voytek, Landor Associates **Photographer:** John Mierisch

Design Firm: Philippe Becker Design, San Francisco CA **Client:** Frantoio **Title:** Olive Oil Bottle **Art Director:** Philippe Becker **Designer:** Philippe Becker

Design Firm: Philippe Becker Design, San Francisco CA **Client:** Buddy Rhodes Studio **Title:** Concrete Counter Mix **Art Director:** Philippe Becker **Designer:** Philippe Becker **Illustrator:** Scott Sawyer

Design Firm: Polan & Waski LLC, Great Neck NY **Client:** Stevens Point Brewery **Title:** Point, Honey Light and White Beers **Designers:** Cathy Szetu, Kathryn Casey **Illustrator:** Tom Nachreiner

Design Firm: Polaroid Corporation, Waltham MA **Title:** One Packaging **Art Director:** Christen K. Gobin **Designer:** Debenham Design, Christen K. Gobin **Photographer:** Gary Sloan

Design Firm: Pouncey Design, Marietta GA **Client:** Southern Beverage
Title: Crystalline Fruit Drinks **Art Director:** Tony Pouncey **Designer:** Tony Pouncey
3D Digital Imaging: Parallax Digital, Atlanta GA

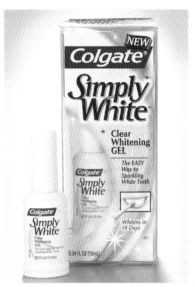

Design Firm: S2 Design Group, New York NY **Client:** Colgate Palmolive
Title: Simply White **Art Director:** Eileen Strauss **Designer:** Eileen Strauss
Photographer: Lori Anzalone

Design Firm: S2 Design Group, New York NY **Client:** Colgate Palmolive
Title: Speed Stick 24/7 **Art Director:** Eileen Strauss **Designer:** Eileen Strauss

Design Firm: S2 Design Group, NY NY **Client:** Colgate Palmolive **Title:** Foamworks
Art Director: Eileen Strauss **Designer:** Eileen Strauss **Illustrator:** Tom Montini

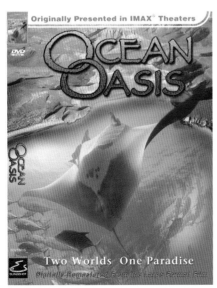

Design Firm: Slingshot Entertainment, Burbank CA **Client:** Summerhays Films
Title: Ocean Oasis **Designer:** Kimberly Conary Russo

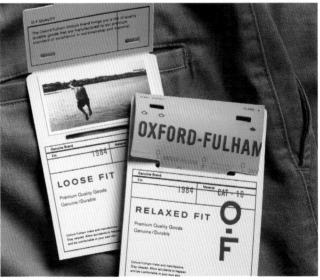

Design Firm: Templin Brink Design, San Francisco CA **Client:** Marshall Fields
Title: Oxford-Fulham Branding/Packaging **Art Directors:** Joel Templin, Gaby Brink
Designer: Brian Gunderson

Design Firm: Templin Brink Design, San Francisco CA **Client:** Target Stores
Title: Merona Branding/Packaging **Art Directors:** Joel Templin, Gaby Brink
Designer: Brian Gunderson

Design Firm: The Bailey Group, Plymouth Meeting PA **Client:** William
Grant & Sons **Title:** Armadale Package Design **Art Directors:** Steve Perry,
Dave Fiedler **Designer:** Layne Lyons

Design Firm: The Bailey Group, Plymouth Meeting PA **Client:** Old Orchard
Title: Package Redesign **Art Directors:** Steve Perry, Dave Fiedler **Designer:** Steve Perry

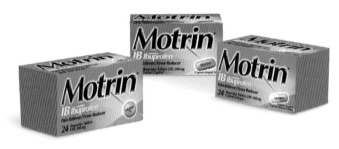

Design Firm: The Bailey Group, Plymouth Meeting PA **Client:** McNeil Consumer
Products **Title:** Motrin Package Design **Art Directors:** Dave Fiedler, Bob Fucinato
Designers: Bob Fucinato, Gary LaCroix

Design Firm: The Stanley Works Inhouse Design Department, New Britain CT
Client: Stanley Works-Woodworking Tools Division **Title:** Bailey Plane Custom Wooden
Box Packaging **Art Director:** Randy Richards **Designers:** Randy Richards, Daren Eddy
Illustrator: David Schulz **Photographer:** Bruno Ratensperger

Design Firm: Thompson Design Group, San Francisco CA **Client:** Freemark Abbey
Title: Freemark Abbey Single-Vineyard Package Design **Art Director:** Dennis
Thompson **Designer:** Felicia Utomo

Design Firm: Twinlab Design Group, Hauppauge NY **Client:** Twinlab
Title: Sports Line **Art Director:** Lauren Smith **Designer:** Lauren Smith

Design Firm: Twinlab Design Group, Hauppauge NY **Client:** Twinlab
Title: XE XA Line **Art Director:** Lauren Smith **Designer:** Chris Harri

Design Firm: Unglued, Scranton PA **Client:** Mighty Fine Wine **Title:** Now Hear This **Art Director:** Jo Ann Wegleski **Designer:** Jo Ann Wegleski

Design Firm: William Fox Munroe, Shillington PA **Client:** R. M. Palmer Candy Co.
Title: Choceur Easter Packaging **Art Director:** Brian Harper **Designer:** Michael Amole

Design Firm: William Fox Munroe, Shillington PA **Client:** Hershey Foods **Title:** To Go!
Packaging **Art Director:** Scott Houtz **Designers:** Michael Amole, Richard Bowersox

Design Firm: William Fox Munroe, Shillington PA **Client:** Hershey Foods
Title: Pretzel Bites Packaging **Art Director:** Brian Harper **Designers:** Rick Rhoades,
Richard Bowersox

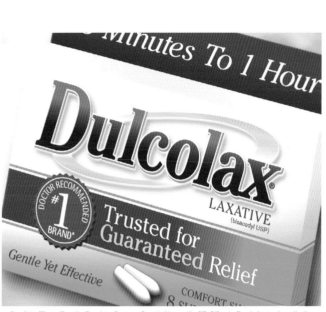

Design Firm: Zunda Design Group, South Norwalk CT **Client:** Boehringer Ingelheim
Title: Dulcolax Laxative **Art Director:** Charles Zunda **Designer:** Todd Nickel

Design Firm: Zunda Design Group, South Norwalk CT **Client:** Hill's Pet Nutrition
Title: Nature's Best Pet Food **Art Directors:** Charles Zunda, Mark Isenhardt
Designer: Todd Nickel

Design Firm: Zunda Design Group, South Norwalk CT **Client:** Pinnacle Foods
Title: Vlasic Pickle Redesign **Art Director:** Charles Zunda **Designer:** Todd Nickel

P-O-P | SIGNS | DISPLAYS | EXHIBITS

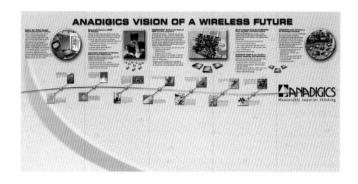

Design Firm: Anadigics, Flanders NJ **Title:** Vision of Wireless Future **Art Director:** John Proaño **Designer:** John Proaño **Photographer:** John Proaño

Design Firm: Arketype Inc., Green Bay WI **Client:** Europharma **Title:** Renouvelle Point-of-Sale **Art Director:** Jim Rivett **Designer:** Matt Bellisle

Design Firm: Bradley & Montgomery Advertising, Indianapolis IN **Client:** Interior Translation **Title:** Elegance **Art Director:** Scott Montgomery

Design Firm: Catalpha Advertising & Design, Towson MD **Client:** SECU Credit Union **Title:** Put Our Low Loan Rates To Work For You Series **Art Director:** Karen Kerski **Designers:** Kolleen Kilduff, Teresa Kowalcyzk

Design Firm: Creative AIM, Southport CT **Client:** Sodexho **Title:** Breakfast to Go **Art Director:** Susan Ripke **Designer:** Denise Arsenault **Illustrator:** Heidi Stevens

Design Firm: Creative Dynamics Inc., Las Vegas NV **Client:** Sony Computer Entertainment America **Title:** Jet X$_2$O Campaign **Art Director:** Victor Rodriguez **Designer:** Eddie Roberts

Design Firm: Creative Options, Edwardsville IL **Client:** Vantage Credit Union
Title: Coin Machine **Designer:** Sherrie Hickman

Design Firm: DCI Marketing, Milwaukee WI **Client:** Cadillac **Title:** Cadillac
Vehicle Portraits **Art Director:** Tom Bruckbauer **Designer:** Tom Bruckbauer
Illustrator: Erika Werych

Design Firm: Design360 Inc./Something Digital Llc., New York NY
Client: Brown Brothers Harriman **Title:** History Exhibit Mural
Art Director: Don Kiel **Designer:** Amanda Hecko

Design Firm: Dever Designs, Laurel MD **Client:** Melwood **Title:** Exhibit
Art Director: Jeffrey L. Dever **Designer:** Jeffrey L. Dever

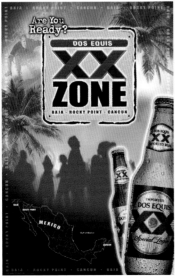

Design Firm: DVC Worldwide, Morristown NJ **Client:** Labatt, USA
Title: Dos Equis XX Zone **Art Director:** Jen Hannon

Design Firm: G2 Worldwide, New York NY **Client:** The Absolut Spirits Company
Title: Absolut Garnish Tray **Art Director:** Andrew Kibble **Designer:** David Dear

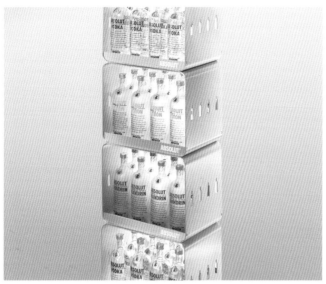

Design Firm: G2 Worldwide, New York NY **Client:** The Absolut Spirits Company
Title: Absolut Modular Floor Rack **Art Director:** Andrew Kibble **Designer:** Hlynur
Atlason **Photographer:** Martin Wonnacott

Design Firm: G2 Worldwide, New York NY **Client:** The Absolut Spirits Company
Title: Absolut Candle Menus **Art Director:** Michael Clarke **Designer:** Maria Samodra
Photographer: Martin Wonnacott

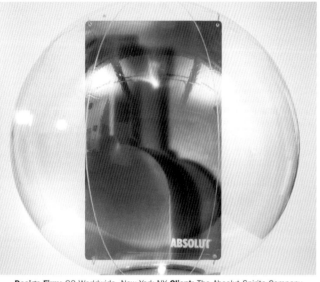

Design Firm: G2 Worldwide, New York NY **Client:** The Absolut Spirits Company
Title: Absolut Inflatable Display **Art Director:** Andrew Kibble **Designer:** Andrew
Kibble **Photographer:** Martin Wonnacott

Design Firm: G2 Worldwide, New York NY **Client:** The Absolut Spirits Company
Title: Absolut Ceiling Danglers **Art Director:** Andrew Kibble **Designer:** Maria Samodra
Photographer: Martin Wonnacott

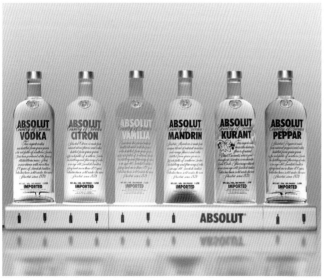

Design Firm: G2 Worldwide, New York NY **Client:** The Absolut Spirits Company
Title: Absolut Pedestal **Art Director:** Michael Clarke **Designer:** Hlynur Atlason
Photographer: Martin Wonnacott

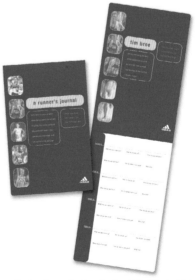

Design Firm: Hanlon Brown Design, Portland OR **Client:** Adidas **Title:** Kid's Log
Book For Boston Marathon **Art Director:** Sandy Brown **Designer:** Anita Wente

P-O-P, SIGNS, DISPLAYS AND EXHIBITS

Design Firm: Island Oasis, Walpole MA **Title:** Feel Good Smoothie P-O-P
Art Director: Peter Buhler **Designer:** Jennifer Howard

Design Firm: Launch Creative Marketing, Hillside IL **Client:** Kellogg/Keebler
Title: LPGA Event **Art Director:** Bill Meier **Designer:** Bill Meier

Design Firm: Launch Creative Marketing, Hillside IL **Client:** Keebler Company
Title: Holiday House Lobby Display **Art Director:** Michelle Morales **Designer:** Michelle
Morales **Illustrators:** Harry Moore (house & elves), Michael Bast (product)

Design Firm: Launch Creative Marketing, Hillside IL **Client:** Keebler Company
Title: Sports Themed Lobby Displays Campaign **Art Directors:** Don Dzielinski, Michelle
Morales **Designers:** Don Dzielinski, Michelle Morales **Illustrator:** James Shepard

Design Firm: Lorenc+Yoo Design, Roswell GA **Client:** Palladium **Title:** Tradeshow
Exhibit **Art Director:** Jan Lorenc **Designers:** Sakchai Rangsiyakorn, Steve McCall
Photographer: Rion Rizzo

Design Firm: Lorenc+Yoo Design, Roswell GA **Client:** Wycliffe **Title:** WordSpring
Discovery Center **Art Director:** Jan Lorenc **Designers:** Chung Yoo, David Park,
Steve McCall **Photographer:** Lee McKee

Design Firm: Lorenc+Yoo Design, Roswell GA Client: Phillips Edison
Title: Tradeshow Exhibit Art Director: Jan Lorenc Designers: Sakchai Rangsiyakorn,
Steve McCall, David Park Photographer: Rion Rizzo

Design Firm: NHL Creative Services, New York NY Client: NHL Events &
Entertainment Title: NHL All Star Enviromental Graphics
Art Directors: Paul Conway, Kathy Drew Designer: Paul Conway

Design Firm: Page Design Inc., Sacramento CA Client: Capitol Racing
Title: Fall Billboard Series Art Director: Paul Page Designer: Chris Brown
Illustrator: Kurt Kland Photographer: Rudy Meyers Photography

Design Firm: Polaroid Corporation, Waltham MA Title: One P-O-P
Art Director: Christen K. Gobin Designer: Christen K. Gobin, Debenham Design
Photographer: Gary Sloan

Design Firm: Proverb Associates, Palos Heights IL Client: Republic Bank
Title: Bank Financial Center Interior Designer: Michael Piper

Design Firm: Rule29, Elgin IL Client: Tyndale House Publishers
Title: iLumina Point- Of-Purchase Art Directors: Justin Ahrens, Jim Bobori
Designers: Justin Ahrens, Jim Bobori

P-O-P, SIGNS, DISPLAYS AND EXHIBITS

Design Firm: Studioeec, West Chester PA **Client:** Studioeec
Title: Trade Show Booth **Art Director:** Jorge Del Fabbro
Designers: Kate Hunsinger, Ken Cox

Design Firm: The Jones Payne Group, Boston MA **Title:** Conference Display
Art Director: Rita Smith **Designers:** Cheryl Gurvich, Peter Raneri

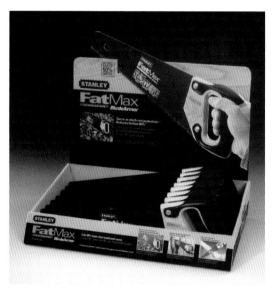

Design Firm: The Stanley Works Inhouse Design Department, New Britain CT
Client: The Stanley Works-Cutting Division **Title:** FatMax Saw Preview Dealer Display
Art Director: Randy Richards **Designers:** Randy Richards, Rick Hart
Photographer: Bruno Ratensperger

Design Firm: The Stanley Works Inhouse Design Department, New Britain CT
Client: The Stanley Works-Cutting Division **Title:** Sport Utility Outdoorsman Knife
Art Director: Randy Richards **Designers:** Dan Deming, Rick Hart, Jon Miller, Randy
Richards **Illustrator:** Dan Deming **Photographer:** Bruno Ratensperger

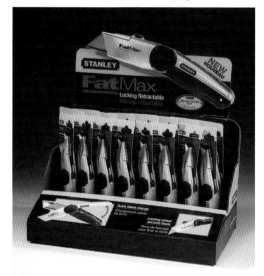

Design Firm: The Stanley Works Inhouse Design Department, New Britain CT
Client: The Stanley Works-Cutting Division **Title:** FatMax Knife Preview Dealer Display
Art Director: Randy Richards **Designers:** Rick Hart, Melissa Garrett
Illustrator: Rick Hart **Photographer:** Bruno Ratensperger

Design Firm: The Stanley Works Inhouse Design Department, New Britain CT
Client: The Stanley Works-Measuring Division **Title:** PowerLock Tape Preview Dealer
Display **Art Director:** Randy Richards **Designers:** Rick Hart, Melissa Garrett
Illustrator: Randy Richards **Photographer:** Bruno Ratensperger

Design Firm: The Stanley Works Inhouse Design Department, New Britain CT
Client: The Stanley Works-Layout Tool Division **Title:** Stud Sensor Preview Dealer
Display **Art Director:** Randy Richards **Designers:** Randy Richards, Rick Hart
Illustrator: Dan Deming **Photographer:** Bruno Ratensperger

Design Firm: Wallach Glass Studio, Santa Rosa CA **Client:** Sutter Cancer Center
Title: The Ranells Family **Art Director:** Christina Wallach **Designer:** Christina Wallach
Illustrator: Arlene Rhoden **Photographer:** Wallach Glass Studio

Design Firm: Wallach Glass Studio, Santa Rosa CA **Client:** St. John's
Cancer Center **Title:** Lower Columbia Regional Cancer Center Donor Wall
Art Director: Christina Wallach **Designer:** Christina Wallach
Illustrator: Arlene Rhoden **Photographer:** Wallach Glass Studio

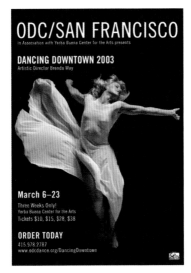

POSTERS

Design Firm: Blue Cross Blue Shield of Texas, Richardson TX Client: Blue Cross Blue Shield of Texas-Abilene Title: Taking Care of Texans Banner
Art Director: Weeda Hamdan Designer: Cynthia Steele

Design Firm: Bradley & Montgomery Advertising, Indianapolis IN
Client: Indie500 Records Title: Behind The Music
Art Director: Scott Montgomery Copywriter: Carrie Voorhis

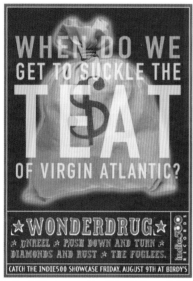

Design Firm: Bradley & Montgomery Advertising, Indianapolis IN Client: Indie500
Records Title: TEAT Art Director: Scott Montgomery Copywriter: Carrie Voorhis

Design Firm: Bradley & Montgomery Advertising, Indianapolis IN Client: Indie500
Records Title: Someday Music Won't Matter Art Director: Scott Montgomery

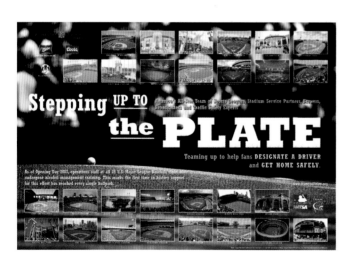

Design Firm: Buck Consultants, St. Louis MO Client: Anheuser-Busch Companies
Title: Stepping Up To the Plate Art Director: Stan Sams Designer: Jennifer Sagaser
Photographers: Major League Baseball and Icon Sports Media

Design Firm: Carbon Smolan Agency, New York NY Client: Morgan Stanley
Title: Leonardo DaVinci: Master Drafstman Art Director: Carla Miller
Designer: Melanie Wiesenthal

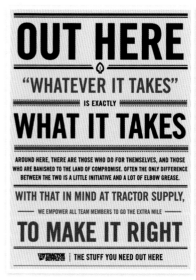

Design Firm: Carmichael Lynch Thorburn, Minneapolis MN Client: Tractor Supply Company Title: What It Takes Creative Director: Bill Thorburn Designer: Charlie Ross

Design Firm: Furst Impressions, Brooklyn NY Client: RVLP Productions Title: Howl Designer: Jessica Furst Photographer: Robert Palmer

Design Firm: International Paper, Memphis TN Title: PMA Expo Souvenir Poster Art Director: Roger Rasor Designers: Shea Morgan, Roger Rasor Illustrator: Shea Morgan

Design Firm: International Paper, Memphis TN Title: Poultry Expo Souvenir Poster Art Director: Roger Rasor Designers: Shea Morgan, Roger Rasor Illustrator: Ross Young

Design Firm: John Townsend Graphic Design, Kalamazoo MI Client: Kalamazoo College Title: What Matters To Me Series Designer: John Townsend

Design Firm: Minx Design, Akron OH Client: Cuyahoga Valley National Park Title: Discover CVNP by Train Designer: Cecilia M. Sveda Illustrator: Cecilia M. Sveda

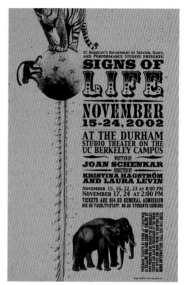

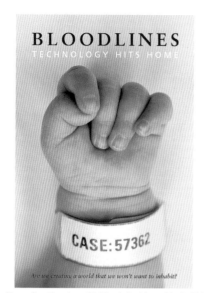

Design Firm: Noon, San Francisco CA Client: UC Berkeley Center for Theater Arts
Title: Signs of Life Art Director: Cinthia Wen Designer: Claudia Fung

Design Firm: Noon, San Francisco CA Client: Backbone Media Title: Bloodlines
Art Director: Cinthia Wen Designer: Claudia Fung

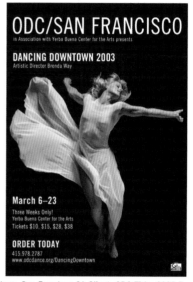

Design Firm: Noon, San Francisco CA Client: ODC Title: 2003 Dancing Downtown
Art Director: Cinthia Wen Designer: Ellen Malinowski

Design Firm: Northeastern University, Boston MA Client: Center for the Arts
Title: Artstuff Poster Art Director: Mary Beth McSwigan Designer: Alicia O'Neill

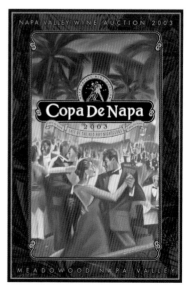

Design Firm: Philippe Becker Design, San Francisco CA Client: Napa Valley
Vintners Association Title: Copa de Napa Poster Art Director: Philippe Becker
Designers: Philippe Becker, Jay Cabalquinto Illustrator: Russ Wilson

Design Firm: Port Of Seattle, Seattle WA Title: The Charles Blood
Award Poster Designer: Dane Fukumoto

Design Firm: Sayles Graphic Design, Des Moines IA **Client:** Ann Arbor Michigan Ad Club **Title:** John Sayles & Sheree Clark A Perfect Fit **Art Director:** John Sayles **Designer:** Som Inthalangsy **Illustrator:** John Sayles

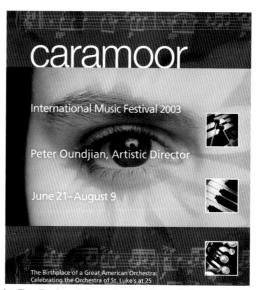

Design Firm: The Barnett Group, New York NY **Client:** Caramoor Center for the Arts **Title:** Festival Transit Poster **Art Directors:** Brian Stern, David Barnett **Designer:** Brian Stern **Photographers:** Henry Wolf and various

Design Firm: The Humane Society of the United States, Gaithersburg MD **Client:** The Humane Society of the Unitied States **Title:** Psst...I have a secret **Art Director:** Paula Jaworski **Designer:** Paula Jaworski

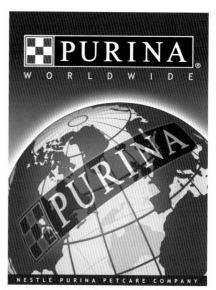

Design Firm: Thompson Design Group, San Francisco CA **Client:** Nestlé Purina PetCare **Title:** Nestlé Purina Poster **Art Director:** Dennis Thompson **Designers:** Dennis Thompson, Gene Dupont

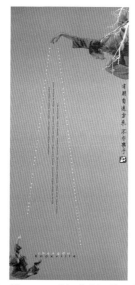

Design Firm: University of Tennessee School of Art, Knoxville TN **Client:** Dogwood Arts Festival/University of Tennessee School of Art **Title:** China Posters **Art Director:** Cary Staples **Illustrator:** Bao Ying

Design Firm: U.S. General Accounting Office, Washington DC **Title:** Diversity Month Campaign **Art Director:** Tony Jasper **Designer:** Tony Jasper

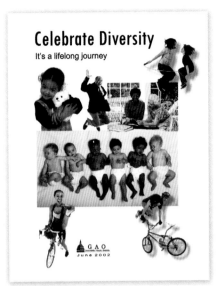

Design Firm: U.S. General Accounting Office, Washington DC **Title:** Diversity Month Campaign **Art Director:** Tony Jasper **Designer:** Tony Jasper

Design Firm: Volume Design, San Francisco CA **Client:** AIGA San Francisco **Title:** 2003 Enrichment Scholarship Poster **Designers:** Adam Brodsley, Eric Heiman **Photographers:** Adam Brodsley, Eric Heiman

PUBLIC SERVICE AND PRO BONO

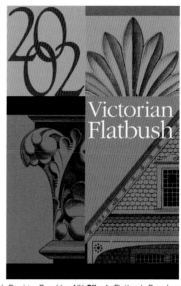

Design Firm: Alberici Group, St. Louis MO **Client:** Cardinal Ritter High School **Title:** Donor Solicitation **Art Director:** Tara Harrison **Designer:** Scott Tripp **Photographers:** Various

Design Firm: Ark Design, Brooklyn NY **Client:** Flatbush Development Corporation **Title:** Neighborhood Guidebook Cover **Designer:** Amanda Kavanagh

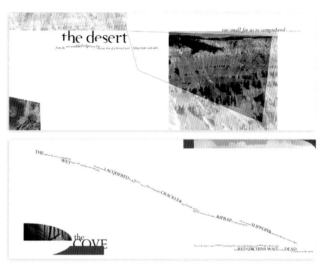

Design Firm: Behan Communications, Glens Falls NY **Client:** Adirondack Tobacco Free Network **Title:** Mass Transit Interior & Exterior Signs Campaign **Art Director:** Troy Burns **Designer:** Troy Burns

Design Firm: C. Sogard Visual Think, Salt Lake City Utah **Client:** Entrada Institute **Title:** Desert Poems Book Project **Art Director:** Carol Sogard **Designer:** Carol Sogard

Design Firm: Cochran + Associates, Chicago IL **Client:** Susan G. Komen Breast Cancer Foundation **Title:** Pink Ribbon Gala Materials **Art Director:** Bobbye Cochran **Designer:** Bobbye Cochran **Illustrator:** Bobbye Cochran

Design Firm: Creative Options, Edwardsville IL **Client:** Metro Community Church **Title:** Changing Lives Brochure **Designer:** Sherrie Hickman

Design Firm: DVC Worldwide, Morristown NJ **Client:** AT&T **Title:** Steven A. Cox Charity Classic **Art Director:** Phil Zusi **Photographers:** Jerry Pinkus, Evan Pinkus

Design Firm: Epstein Design Partners, Cleveland OH **Client:** XPEDX **Title:** Fall Paper Preview Invite **Designer:** Brian Jasinski **Illustrator:** Doug Goldsmith

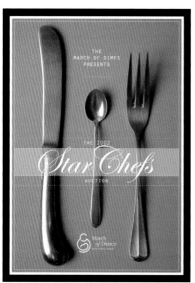

Design Firm: Faith Design, Mamaroneck NY **Client:** Men's Fellowship of the New Canaan Congregational Church **Title:** Benefit for Sports Outreach Program **Art Director:** Faith E. Deegan **Designer:** Faith E. Deegan **Photographer:** Faith E. Deegan

Design Firm: Flourish, Cleveland OH **Client:** The March Of Dimes **Title:** 2002 All Star Chefs Auction **Art Directors:** Christopher Ferranti, Jing Lauengco, Henry Frey **Designer:** Steve Shuman **Photographer:** Steve Shuman

Design Firm: Griffith Phillips Creative, Dallas TX **Client:** Salvation Army of North Texas **Title:** Annual Report **Designer:** Brian Niemann **Photographer:** Pete Lacker

Design Firm: ING Marketing Department, Hartford CT **Client:** The Connecticut Opera **Title:** Pavarotti Invitation **Designer:** ING Marketing Department

Design Firm: Intelligent Fish Studio, Palatine IL **Client:** Andrea Haberman Benefit **Title:** Poster **Art Director:** Brian Danaher **Designers:** Brian Danaher, Natalie Danaher **Illustrator:** Brian Danaher

Design Firm: Ison Design, San Francisco CA **Client:** Planned Parenthood Golden Gate **Title:** Luncheon Invitation **Designer:** Annabelle Ison

Design Firm: K. McGilvery Design, New York NY **Client:** Puppies Behind Bars **Title:** Semi-Annual Newsletter **Art Director:** Kathy McGilvery **Designer:** Kathy McGilvery **Photographers:** Various

Design Firm: Kelly Design Company, Hartford CT **Client:** Greater Hartford Arts Council **Title:** Progress Report **Art Director:** Bill Kelly **Designer:** Roxanne Kelly **Photographers:** Robert Reichert and various

Design Firm: Morehead Dotts & Associates, Corpus Christi TX **Client:** American Diabetes Association, Corpus Christi TX **Title:** Event Logo **Designer:** Roy Smith

Design Firm: Phoenix Creative Group, Herndon VA **Client:** Arena Stage **Title:** Phantom Ball Fundraiser Invitation **Art Director:** Nicole Kassolis

Design Firm: Rock-Tenn Company, Norcross GA **Client:** The Bridge **Title:** Spring 2003 Newsletter **Art Director:** Greg Vaughn **Designer:** Greg Vaughn

Design Firm: Southern Company, Atlanta GA **Clients:** Barnsley Gardens Inn & Resort and Southern Co. **Title:** Rescue 3 Charity Benefit **Art Director:** Vicki Gardocki **Designer:** Amy McGurk

Design Firm: VMA Inc., Dayton OH **Client:** Cincinnati Ballet **Title:** Logo
Art Director: Kenneth Botts **Designer:** Joel Warneke **Photographer:** Patrick Jennings

Design Firm: ZGraphics Ltd., East Dundee IL **Client:** One Small Voice Foundation **Title:** 2002 Open Toe Shoe Party Invite **Art Director:** LouAnn Zeller **Designer:** Renee Clark

SALES PROMOTION

Design Firm: Arketype Inc., Green Bay WI Client: Gilbert Paper Title: ID
Art Director: Jim Rivett Designer: Matt Bellisle Illustrators: Matt Bellisle, DeGaull
Vang, Robb Mommaerts Photographers: Arketype Inc. and Image Studios

Design Firm: Brandscope, Chicago IL Client: Kaleidoscope Imaging Title: Capabilities
Promotion Art Directors: William Harper, Kelly Shelton Designer: Tim Quirk

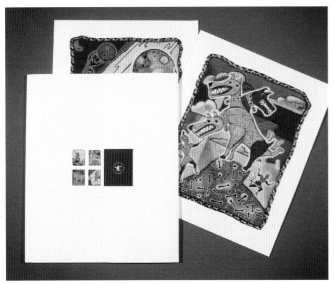

Design Firm: Cisneros Design, Santa Fe NM Client: Imperial Lithograph
Title: Printer-Series Promotion Art Director: Fred Cisneros Designer: Fred Cisneros
Illustrator: Joel Nakamura

Design Firm: G2 Worldwide, New York NY Client: The Absolut Spirits Company
Title: Absolut Sales Kit Art Director: Andrew Kibble Designer: Maria Samodra
Photographer: Martin Wonnacott

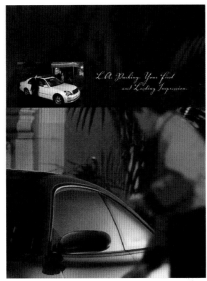

Design Firm: Gary Taylor Creative Group, Los Angeles CA Client: LA Parking Services
Inc. Title: Presentation Folder Art Director: Gary Taylor
Designer: Michael Gonzales Photographer: Paul Rumohr

Design Firm: Gary Taylor Creative Group, Los Angeles CA Client: Kawasaki Motors
Corp. USA Title: Press Kit/Folder Art Director: Gary Taylor Designer: Michael
Gonzales Photographers: Rich Cox, Kevin Wing, Frank Hoppen

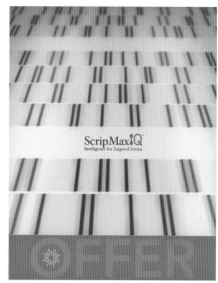

Design Firm: Great Ideas 2 Go, Hunt Valley MD **Client:** The Understanding & Insight Group **Title:** Promo Kit **Art Director:** Diane Hamel **Designer:** Diane Hamel

Design Firm: Greenhouse Design, Highland Park NJ **Client:** Dendrite International **Title:** Sales Promotion **Art Director:** Miriam Grunhaus **Designer:** Miriam Grunhaus

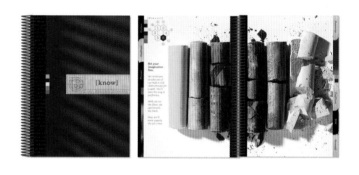

Design Firm: Haymarket Media, Staten Island NY **Client:** Medical Marketing & Media **Title:** Media Kit **Art Director:** Irasema Rivera **Designer:** Irasema Rivera

Design Firm: Hixson Design, Charlotte NC **Client:** Classic Graphics **Title:** know (the classic formula) **Art Director:** Gary Hixson **Designer:** Gary Hixson **Photographer:** Rick Hovis

Design Firm: Inova Health System, Springfield VA **Client:** Inova Workplace Health Services **Title:** Sales Brochure **Art Director:** Rachel Arnold **Designer:** Catalyst Design

Design Firm: Interactive Network for Continuing Education (INCE), Cranbury NJ **Title:** Cutting Edge **Art Director:** Jamie Santiago **Designer:** Jamie Santiago

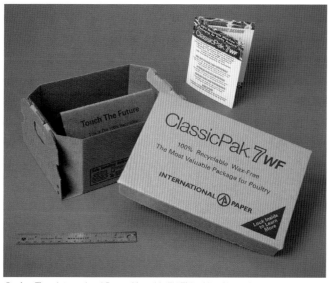

Design Firm: International Paper, Memphis TN **Title:** Mini ClassicPak 7 WF Promotion
Art Director: Roger Rasor **Designer:** Shea Morgan

Design Firm: Island Oasis, Walpole MA **Client:** Long Beach Brewing Co.
Title: Thin Ice T-Shirt **Designer:** Peter Buhler

Design Firm: Kensington Creative Worldwide, Inc., McLean VA
Client: Congressional Quarterly **Title:** Media Kit **Designer:** Jon Saunders

Design Firm: Launch Creative Marketing, Hillside IL **Client:** Saputo USA
Title: Frigo Calendar Promotion **Art Director:** Brian Spain **Designer:** Brian Spain
Photographers: Brian Beaugureau and various

Design Firm: LFM Design, Hillside NJ **Client:** Dr. Patty's Skincare Products **Title:**
Sample Card & Packet **Designer:** Laura F. Menza **Photographer:** Greg LeMar

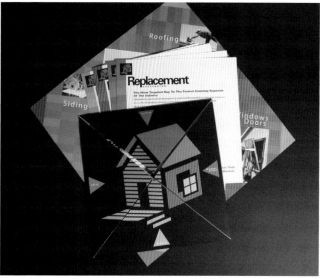

Design Firm: LTD Creative, Frederick MD **Client:** Hanley-Wood, LLC
Title: Replacement Contractor Promo **Art Director:** Louanne Welgoss
Designer: Kimberly Dow **Copywriter:** Melissa Dole

Design Firm: LTD Creative, Frederick MD **Client:** Hanley-Wood, LLC **Title:** Custom Home Kitchen & Bath Promo **Art Director:** Louanne Welgoss **Designer:** Kimberly Dow **Copywriter:** Melissa Dole

Design Firm: LTD Creative, Frederick MD **Client:** Hanley-Wood, LLC **Title:** Remodeling Magazine Media Kit **Art Director:** Timothy Finnen **Designer:** Kimberly Dow

Design Firm: Money Magazine, New York NY **Client:** Money Magazine/Time Inc. **Title:** Media Kit **Art Director:** Cari Colclough

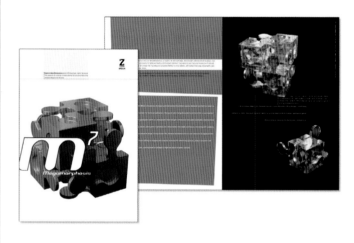

Design Firm: NDW Communications, Horsham PA **Client:** M-real **Title:** M7 (Megamorphosis Issue 7) **Art Director:** Bill Healey **Designer:** Bill Healey **Illustrator:** John Harwood

Design Firm: NDW Communications, Horsham PA **Client:** Fox River Paper **Title:** Coversitility **Art Director:** Tom Brill **Designer:** Tom Brill **Photographer:** Dan Naylor

Design Firm: Page Design Inc., Sacramento CA **Client:** Lowepro **Title:** Sales Promo **Art Director:** Paul Page **Designers:** Heather Orr, Kurt Kland **Illustrators:** Kurt Kland, Chris Brown

Design Firm: Project 03, North Aurora IL **Client:** ONSITE Woodwork Corporation **Title:** Reception Desks **Designer:** Jason Onken, Project 03

Design Firm: Quad Creative Group, Milwaukee WI **Client:** Quad/Photo **Title:** Sales Kit **Art Director:** Tom Campbell **Designers:** Brooke Luteyn, Nancy Buege **Photographer:** Quad/Photo

Design Firm: Reich Paper, Brooklyn NY **Title:** Shine Swatchbook **Art Director:** Drew Souza **Designer:** Drew Souza

Design Firm: Time Magazine/Time Marketing, New York NY **Client:** Time Magazine **Title:** Media Kit **Creative Services Director:** Liza Greene **Art Director:** Mike Iadanza **Photographers:** Various

Design Firm: Tin Yen Studios, Alhambra CA **Client:** Epson America **Title:** Holiday Mailer **Art Directors:** Ching Lau, Tin Yen **Designer:** Ching Lau

Design Firm: Tribune Media Services, Chicago IL **Client:** VUE **Title:** VUE Folder **Art Director:** Jill Sherman **Photographers:** Various

Design Firm: Tribune Media Services, Chicago IL **Client:** VUE
Title: OverVUE Booklet **Art Director:** Jill Sherman **Photographers:** Various

Design Firm: William Fox Munroe, Shillington PA **Client:** Hershey Foods
Title: To Go! Turbo Sales Kit **Art Director:** Scott Houtz **Designer:** Rick Rhoades

Design Firm: Williams and House, Avon CT **Client:** Mohawk Paper Mills **Title:** The
Cover Story **Art Directors:** Robert Valentine, Liddy Walseth, The Valentine Group
Designer: Robert Valentine, The Valentine Group **Copywriters:** Pam Williams, Williams
and House and Walter Thomas, Air Force One **Photographer:** Martyn Thompson NY

Design Firm: Williams and House, Avon CT **Client:** The Artcraft Company
Title: Color on Color 1 **Art Director:** Pam Williams **Designer:** Fred Schaub, Oxford CT
Copywriter: Pam Williams

Design Firm: Woman's Day Creative Services, New York NY **Title:** Woman's Day
Relaunch Promotion **Art Director:** Beth Ann Silvestri **Designer:** Beth Ann Silvestri
Photographers: Peter Freed (publisher's portrait), Luciana Pampalone (magazine cover)

Design Firm: Zinc, New York NY **Client:** Related Residential Development **Title:** The
Tate Tin **Designers:** Peter Maloney, Felicia Zekauskas **Illustrator:** David Cain

SELF PROMOTION

Design Firm: Aaron Design, New York NY **Title:** Self-Promo **Art Director:** Stephanie Aaron **Designer:** Stephanie Aaron

Addison

Design Firm: Addison, New York NY **Title:** Splash **Art Director:** David Kohler **Illustrator:** Chris Yun **Photographers:** Jody Dole, William Vasquez

Design Firm: AJF Marketing, Piscataway NJ **Title:** Properly Positioned **Art Director:** Justin Brindisi **Designer:** Justin Brindisi

Design Firm: ART 270, Jenkintown PA **Title:** Self-Promotion **Art Director:** Carl Mill **Designers:** Sagan Medvec, Nicole Ganz **Photographer:** David Debalko

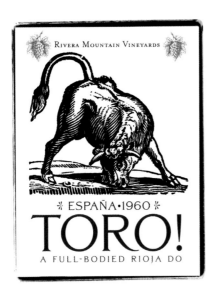

Design Firm: Big I Ranch Design Studio, Staten Island NY **Title:** Toro! **Art Director:** Irasema Rivera **Designer:** Irasema Rivera

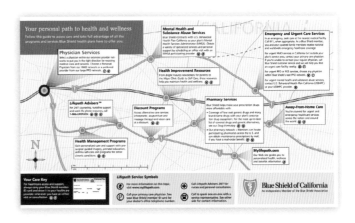

Design Firm: Blue Shield of California, San Francisco CA **Title:** Z Card **Art Director:** Stephanie Donahue **Designer:** Larissa Nahhas **Illustrator:** Larissa Nahhas

Design Firm: Buck Consultants, St. Louis MO Client: Buck Consultants/
LiveWire Media Title: Who's in Your Corner? Art Director: Stan Sams
Designer: Elizabeth Lohmeyer

Design Firm: CAI Communications, Raleigh NC Client: Capital Associated Industries
Title: Promo Art Director: Steve McCulloch Designer: Steve McCulloch

Design Firm: Cisneros Design, Santa Fe NM Title: Holiday Card
Designer: Janine Pearson Photographer: Chris Corrie

Design Firm: CMDS, Middletown NJ Title: Belly-Warming Design!
Art Director: Chris Mulvaney Designer: Chris Mulvaney Illustrator: Chris Mulvaney
Photographer: Chris Mulvaney

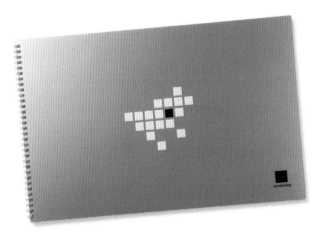

Design Firm: DCI Marketing, Milwaukee WI Title: Client Solicitation Brochure
Art Director: Alan Eliason Designer: Alan Eliason Copywriter: Ric Sorgel, OCI

Design Firm: Deloitte & Touche, Boston MA Title: Recognized for Excellence
Art Director: Barbara Calautti Designer: Natalie Salls

Design Firm: Design North, Racine WI Title: Capabilities Art Director: Gwen
Granzow Designers: Entire Design North Staff Photographer: Peter Hernandez

Design Firm: Dever Designs, Laurel MD Title: It's Not Magic Promotion Card
Art Director: Jeffrey Dever Designer: Jeffrey L. Dever

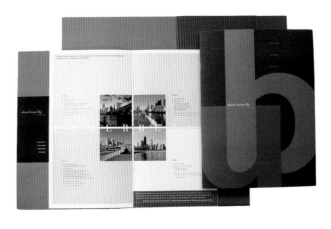

Design Firm: DM.2 Design, Edgewater NJ Title: Voice Brochure
Art Director: Team Designer: Team

Design Firm: Epstein Design Partners, Cleveland OH Client: Ulmer & Berne, LLP
Title: Cincinnati Brochure/Folder Designer: John Okal

Design Firm: Eyeball NYC, New York NY Title: Reel 2003

Design Firm: Ezzona Design Group, Burbank CA Title: Holiday Cards Art Directors:
Gina Vivona, James Pezzullo Designer: Nida Sanger Illustrator: Gina Vivona

Design Firm: Ezzona Design Group, Burbank CA Title: Self Promo Packet
Art Directors: Gina Vivona, James Pezzullo Designer: Nida Sanger
Illustrator: Gina Vivona Photographer: Barry Goyette

Design Firm: Flourish, Cleveland OH Client: Arhaus Furniture Title: April Mailer
Designers: Christopher Ferranti, Charity Ewanko, Henry Frey, Jing Lauchengco

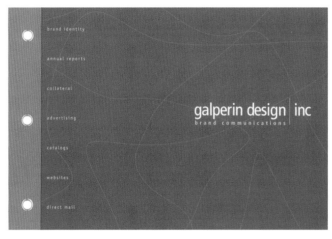

Design Firm: Furst Impressions, Brooklyn NY Title: Happy Designer: Jessica Furst

Design Firm: Galperin Design Inc., New York NY Title: GDI Promotion
Art Director: Peter Galperin Designer: Kristina Paukulis Photographer: Bill White

Design Firm: Glick Design, Kahului HI Title: Portfolio XII Art Director: Robert Glick
Designer: Robert Glick Illustrator: Robert Glick Photographer: Robert Glick

Design Firm: Griffith Phillips Creative, Dallas TX Title: Flake Feast
Art Director: Brian Niemann Designer: Aaron McKee

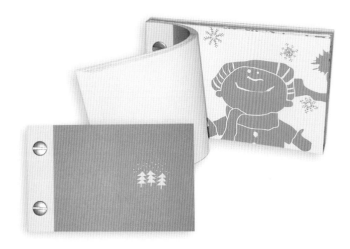

Design Firm: Griffith Phillips Creative, Dallas TX **Title:** The Flippin Book
Art Director: Bo McCord **Designer:** Cord Mitchell

Design Firm: Inova Health System, Springfield VA **Client:** Inova Alexandria
Hospital **Title:** 130th Anniversary Timeline **Art Director:** Rachel Arnold
Designer: Katherine Kwiatkowski

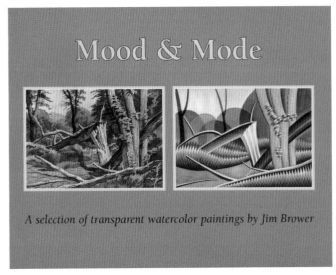

Design Firm: Ion Design, Frederick MD **Title:** Look Book **Art Director:** Ruth
Bielobocky **Designer:** Eryn Willard **Photographers:** Rob Blair and various

Design Firm: Jim Brower Studio, Toledo OH **Title:** Mood and Mode
Art Director: Jim Brower **Designer:** Jim Brower **Illustrator:** Jim Brower

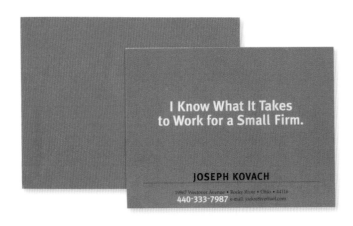

Design Firm: KRE8IVE Design, Cleveland OH **Title:** Self Promotion
Art Director: Joseph S. Kovach **Designer:** Joseph S. Kovach

Design Firm: Multipod, Brooklyn NY **Client:** Liz Lomax **Title:** Liz Lomax 3D Illustration
Art Director: Randi Hazan **Designer:** Randi Hazan **Illustrator:** Liz Lomax

Design Firm: OrangeSeed Design, Minneapolis MN **Title:** Winter Harvest
Art Director: Damien Wolf **Designers:** Damien Wolf, Dale Mustful, Phil Hoch

Design Firm: Pink & White Illustration & Design, Chicago IL **Client:** Pink & White
Illustration & Design **Title:** Promotional Postcard **Art Director:** Heather Schulein
Designer: Heather Schulein **Illustrator:** Heather Schulein

Design Firm: Smizer Design, Waterford CT **Title:** Swimsuit Calendar
Art Director: Karl Smizer **Designer:** Lizann Michaud **Photographer:** Derek Dudek

Design Firm: Smizer Design, Waterford CT **Title:** Tribute to the Best
Art Director: Karl Smizer **Designer:** Mark Dullea **Illustrator:** Mark Dullea

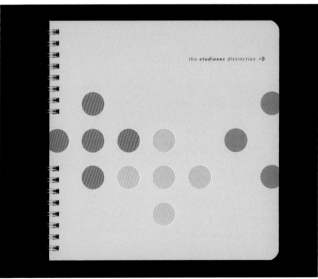

Design Firm: Studio J, North Highlands CA **Title:** Portfolio Sampler
Designer: Angela Jackson **Photographer:** Nina Courtney Photography

Design Firm: Studioeec, West Chester PA **Client:** Studioeec
Title: Studioeec Brochure **Art Director:** Jorge Del Fabbro **Designer:** Kate Hunsinger
Photographer: Jorge Del Fabbro

Design Firm: Talisman Interactive, Philadelphia PA **Client:** Gravica Design
Title: Poster **Creative Director:** Michael McDonald

Design Firm: The College Board, New York NY **Title:** The CLEP Advising Kit
Designers: Meridith Haber and Suka Designs

Design Firm: Wolken Communica, Seattle WA **Client:** Bellevue Art Museum
Title: Scapes **Art Director:** Kurt Wolken **Designer:** Ryan Burlinson
Illustrator: Darren Waterson

Design Firm: Yamamoto Moss, Minneapolis MN **Client:** Dare to
Breathe **Title:** Promotion **Art Director:** Alan Tse **Designer:** Alan Tse
Photographer: Stephanie Colgan

FIRMS REPRESENTED